James Du Buisson

The origin and peculiar characteristics of the Gospel of S.

Mark

1896

James Du Buisson

The origin and peculiar characteristics of the Gospel of S. Mark
1896

ISBN/EAN: 9783337284084

Printed in Europe, USA, Canada, Australia, Japan

Cover: Foto ©Andreas Hilbeck / pixelio.de

More available books at **www.hansebooks.com**

The Origin and Peculiar Characteristics of the Gospel of S. Mark, and its Relation to the other Synoptists, Being the Ellerton Essay

1896

BY

J. C. DU BUISSON, B.A.

LATE DEMY OF MAGDALEN COLLEGE

Oxford

AT THE CLARENDON PRESS

1896

CONTENTS

PART I.

ORIGIN OF THE GOSPEL.

PART II.

RELATION TO THE OTHER SYNOPTISTS.

PART III.

PURPOSE AND CHARACTERISTICS OF THE GOSPEL.

The Origin and Peculiar Characteristics of the Gospel of S. Mark.

PART I.

The Origin of the Gospel.

FOR nearly eighteen centuries the Gospel of S. Mark met with comparative neglect at the hands of theologians. Only one patristic commentary, the Catena, has come down to us. Writers who have commented on all four Gospels have in most cases, when treating of S. Mark, been content to refer their readers to the parallel passages in S. Matthew or S. Luke. And the reason of this neglect is not far to seek. Alike to theologian and to critic the second Gospel, in comparison with the other three, seems to offer but scanty material for study. To one familiar with the other Synoptists the Marcan account of our Lord's life, with its omission of the story of His birth and infancy, of the details of the Temptation, of the Sermon on the Mount, of the Lord's Prayer, and of the majority of the parables, naturally leaves the impression of poverty and incompleteness. · Nor from a critical and literary point of view did the Gospel fare any better. The fact that the second Evangelist records little that is not also found in the other Synoptical Gospels led S. Augustine to regard him as a mere follower and epitomist of S. Matthew, and the verdict of the great African father was until quite recent years generally acquiesced in [1].

Introductory. Former neglect of S. Mark's Gospel.

---

[1] Aug. *De Cons. Ev.* i. 4. Marcus Matthaeum subsecutus, tamquam pedisequus et breviator eius videtur.

Even the rise of modern criticism did not for a considerable time effect any change in the place accorded to S. Mark. One of the earliest of modern critical writers, Griesbach, pronounced it to be an epitome not only of S. Matthew but of the other two Gospels as well, and this view was endorsed by Baur and his followers, so that only when the general revolt against the Tübingen school took place did there follow the inevitable reaction in favour of the second Gospel. The pendulum swung round, and there arose a tendency to find in S. Mark not the latest but the earliest of the Gospels. Hence special attention was directed to it, for it was felt that the settlement of the questions of its date and of its relation to S. Matthew and S. Luke would go far towards the solution of the whole Synoptic problem.

Quite apart also from critical considerations the Gospel of S. Mark has a peculiar beauty and attractiveness of its own, which the keen scrutiny demanded by modern methods of study has but brought into greater prominence. The plain, straightforward narrative, enriched at the same time with a wealth of vivid detail, seems to bear on it the stamp of personal recollections; so that even regarded merely as a biographical memoir the Gospel has all the interest which attaches to the testimony of an eye-witness. Theologically considered, S. Mark presents in the simplest and most direct form 'the Gospel of Jesus Christ the Son of God,' depicting Him as the Divine Man living and working among His fellow-men, and thus giving greater prominence to His acts than to His words. It is essentially a practical Gospel, admirably adapted to the practical genius of the Roman Christians to whom, according to ancient tradition, it was addressed. If it does not attain to the theological heights of S. John, this is only in accordance with the law of progressive revelation. The history of our Lord's life, death, and resurrection had to be firmly established before men were fit to receive the loftier spiritual truths deduced from those facts in the pages of the fourth Gospel [1].

The general consensus of opinion in favour of assigning an early date to S. Mark's Gospel lends a special interest to the consideration of the circumstances of its origin. Why is the second Gospel known as the Gospel according to S. Mark, seeing that his name is not mentioned in it, and that there is no internal evidence to prove that he is the author? The question is answered by the unanimous voice of early tradition, which attributes the authorship to the 'John whose surname is Mark' of whom we read in the Acts of the Apostles [2]. And tradition does not stop here, but goes on to tell us something of the circumstances under which the Gospel was composed. The first witness, both in order of time and in the intrinsic importance of his testimony, is Papias, bishop of Hierapolis in Phrygia, who wrote c. A.D. 130–140 a work entitled *Expositions of Oracles of the Lord*, fragments of which have been preserved in the ecclesiastical history of Eusebius. Papias forms a direct link with the apostolic age, having been a 'hearer' of 'John the Elder,' who was himself 'a disciple of the Lord.' The following are the words relating to S. Mark which are quoted by Eusebius: 'And the Elder said this also. Mark, having become the interpreter of Peter, wrote down accurately everything that he remembered, without however recording in order what was either said or done by Christ. For neither did he hear the Lord, nor did he follow Him; but afterwards, as I said, [attended] Peter, who adapted his instructions to the needs [of his hearers], but had no design of giving a connected account of the Lord's oracles. So then Mark made no mistake, while he thus wrote down some things as he remembered them; for he made it his one care not to omit anything that he heard, or to set down any false statement therein [3].'

[margin: Origin of the Gospel.
I. Traditional accounts.
(1) Second century authorities.
Papias.]

---

[1] Cf Wright, *Composition of the Four Gospels*, c. v.   [2] Acts xii. 25.
[3] Eus. *H. E.* iii. 39 καὶ τοῦτο ὁ πρεσβύτερος ἔλεγε· Μάρκος μὲν ἑρμηνευτὴς

Few passages of any writer ancient or modern have given rise to so much controversy as this fragment. As will be seen hereafter, it presents some difficulties which in the absence of the complete work of Papias may remain unsolved, but it is sufficient here to notice what is after all the main fact which it attests, namely, the intimate connexion between S. Mark and S. Peter. This is borne out by the witness of later writers, while differences in detail show that their statements are not based merely on the authority of Papias. Some of the notices are very obscure, and it is difficult to prove conclusively their reference to our Gospel of S. Mark, although the balance of evidence seems to point in that direction.

Justin Martyr.   Justin Martyr (150–165) mentions the name Boanerges given to the sons of Zebedee, and adds that Christ changed the name of one of the Apostles to Peter, and that this is 'written in his memoirs[1].' Since S. Mark is the only Evangelist who records the name Boanerges, it would be a natural inference that the ἀπομνημονεύματα Πέτρου is only the second Gospel under another name. On the other hand a different conclusion has been suggested by recent events. The recovery in 1887 from an Egyptian tomb of a fragment of the apocryphal 'Gospel of Peter' has brought before us the possibility that Justin is here referring to that work, and not to a canonical writing at all. This view is borne out by certain points in the language of the first Apology and Dialogue, which seem to imply a knowledge of the Gospel[2]. Unfortunately the

---

Πέτρου γενόμενος, ὅσα ἐμνημόνευσεν, ἀκριβῶς ἔγραψεν, οὐ μέντοι τάξει, τὰ ὑπὸ τοῦ Χριστοῦ ἢ λεχθέντα ἢ πραχθέντα. οὔτε γὰρ ἤκουσε τοῦ Κυρίου. οὔτε παρηκολούθησεν αὐτῷ, ὕστερον δέ, ὡς ἔφην, Πέτρῳ, ὃς πρὸς τὰς χρείας ἐποιεῖτο τὰς διδασκαλίας, ἀλλ᾽ οὐχ ὥσπερ σύνταξιν τῶν κυριακῶν ποιούμενος λογίων, ὥστε οὐδὲν ἥμαρτε Μᾶρκος, οὕτως ἔνια γράψας ὡς ἀπεμνημόνευσεν. ἑνὸς γὰρ ἐποιήσατο πρόνοιαν, τοῦ μηδὲν ὧν ἤκουσε παραλιπεῖν ἢ ψεύσασθαί τι ἐν αὐτοῖς.

[1] *Dial.* c. 106 γεγράφθαι ἐν τοῖς ἀπομνημονεύμασιν αὐτοῦ.

[2] The question whether Justin shows an acquaintance with the Gospel of S. Peter is however still *sub iudice.* Dr. Swete decides, although with hesitation, in the negative. *Gospel of S. Peter,* Introd. pp. xxxiii. f.

recovered fragment contains only the history of the Passion, so that we do not know whether the change of S. Peter's name was recorded in the earlier part of the work.

We stand on firmer ground when we reach Irenaeus Irenaeus. (180-190), who gives more exact information as to the origin and date of the Gospel of S. Mark. 'After the decease of these' (S Peter and S. Paul), he says, 'Mark, the disciple and interpreter of Peter, himself also handed down to us in writing the things which were preached by Peter[1].' There is an alternative reading 'after the publication of this' (S. Matthew's Gospel), which is interesting, as the date which it implies is in harmony with a later tradition, recorded by Origen, that the first Gospel was composed before the second.

The testimony of the Muratorian Canon (c. 200), the Murator-earliest known list of the books of the New Testament, is ian Canon. more fragmentary. The extant portion of the document begins with a few words which evidently conclude a notice of S. Mark, for it proceeds to treat of S. Luke which it calls 'the third book of the Gospel.' The words in question are 'at which nevertheless he was present and so recorded them[2],' and it is generally supposed that the reference is to the Petrine origin of the Gospel, although the absence of the context prevents us from speaking with certainty.

Clement of Alexandria gives an explicit and detailed Clement account, and is the first to connect the Gospel with Rome. of Alex-andria. He states on the authority of 'the elders of a former age' that 'when Peter had publicly preached the word in Rome, and declared the Gospel by the Spirit, those who were present being many exhorted Mark, as one who had followed him for a long time and remembered his words,

---

[1] *Contr. Haer.* III. i. 1 Μετὰ δὲ τὴν τούτων ἔξοδον (al. τούτου ἔκδοσιν) Μάρκος ὁ μαθητὴς καὶ ἑρμηνευτὴς Πέτρου καὶ αὐτὸς τὰ ὑπὸ Πέτρου κηρυσσόμενα ἐγγράφως ἡμῖν παραδέδωκε.

[2] .... quibus tamen interfuit et ita posuit. Tertium Evangelii librum secundum Lucam, &c.

to write down what he said; and he, having made his Gospel, delivered it to those who had asked him, and Peter, when he came to know of it, took pains neither to hinder nor encourage him [1].'

(2) Third century. Tertullian. Origen.

Among writers of the third century Tertullian and Origen carry on the same tradition. The former remarks that 'the Gospel which Mark brought out is maintained to be Peter's, whose interpreter he was [2],' while the latter goes so far as to say that 'Mark made his Gospel as Peter guided him [3].'

(3) Fourth century. Eusebius.

In the fourth century Eusebius tells the same story with further embellishments. His words are worth quoting, as they claim to rest on the authority of Papias and Clement, and also throw light on an interesting passage in the first Epistle of S. Peter. After stating that the Gospel was written by S. Mark in accordance with the wish of S. Peter's disciples to have a written record of the Apostle's teaching, Eusebius proceeds: 'They say that when the Apostle knew what had been done (the Spirit having revealed it to him), he was pleased at the zeal of the men and sanctioned the writing for the use of the Churches (Clement has recorded the story in the sixth book of his *Hypotyposeis*, and Papias, bishop of Hierapolis, gives like testimony): and that Peter makes mention of Mark in his first Epistle, which it is also said that he composed in Rome, and that he himself intimates this by giving the city the metaphorical name of Babylon [4].'

---

[1] Fragm. Hypotyp. 1016 P. in Eus. *H. E.* vi. 14 τοῦ Πέτρου δημοσίᾳ ἐν Ῥώμῃ κηρύξαντος τὸν λόγον καὶ πνεύματι τὸ εὐαγγέλιον ἐξειπόντος, τοὺς παρόντας πολλοὺς ὄντας παρακαλέσαι τὸν Μάρκον, ὡς ἂν ἀκολουθήσαντα αὐτῷ πόρρωθεν καὶ μεμνημένον τῶν λεχθέντων, ἀναγράψαι τὰ εἰρημένα, ποιήσαντα δὲ τὸ εὐαγγέλιον μεταδοῦναι τοῖς δεομένοις αὐτοῦ, ὅπερ ἐπιγνόντα τὸν Πέτρον προτρεπτικῶς μήτε κωλῦσαι μήτε προτρέψασθαι.

[2] *Adv. Marc.* iv. 5 Marcus quod edidit Evangelium Petri affirmatur, cuius interpres Marcus.

[3] Comm. in Mt. 1. Eus. *H. E.* vi. 25 δεύτερον δὲ (εὐαγγέλιον) τὸ κατὰ Μάρκον, ὡς Πέτρος ὑφηγήσατο αὐτῷ ποιήσαντα.

[4] *H. E.* ii. 16.

Beyond Eusebius, the peculiar features of whose account will be subsequently considered, it is not necessary to go. The further we get from the Apostolic age the more apparent it becomes that multiplicity of detail is no guarantee of the accuracy of a tradition, but rather the reverse. The later writers know much more than the earlier about the circumstances under which the Gospel was composed, and it is especially noticeable how as time goes on the influence of the Apostle on the Evangelist is represented as more and more direct. All that can be accepted as really authentic is the general statement that S. Mark composed a Gospel on the basis of S. Peter's preaching. Other details must be received with caution, although some of them, like the statement of Irenaeus as to the date of the Gospel, attain to a high degree of probability. That Irenaeus is in this respect at variance with the general voice of later tradition is not surprising, since it is easy to imagine how the idea that S. Peter himself authorized the composition of the Gospel would grow out of the vague tradition that it was founded on the Petrine teaching.

How far is the traditional view of the origin of the second Gospel borne out by the witness of the New Testament itself? The answer to this question can only be given after an examination of both the external evidence, that is, the notices of S. Mark in the Acts and Epistles, and the internal evidence presented by the contents, structure, and language of the Gospel itself. *II. The witness of the New Testament.*

Taking the external evidence first, we find that we are enabled to construct from various passages a tolerably distinct account of the life of S. Mark, although, as is the case with so many New Testament characters, there are great gaps in his career, which can only be filled up by conjecture. 'John, whose surname was Mark,' was by birth a Jew, and perhaps came of a priestly family, since, as we learn from the Epistle to the Colossians, he was *Notices of S. Mark in Acts and Epistles.*

a cousin of Barnabas, the Levite of Cyprus[1]. His home was at Jerusalem, where his mother's house seems to have been a customary meeting-place for the persecuted members of the early Church. When S. Peter was released from prison by the angel, he at once repaired to this house, where he found many gathered together and praying[2]. In all probability therefore S. Mark was at an early age brought under Christian influences. He soon appears in connexion with S. Paul and S. Barnabas, accompanying them from Jerusalem to Antioch after the fulfilment of their commission to the 'brethren that dwelt in Judaea[3].' At this point his missionary career began. He went with the two Apostles on their first journey in the capacity of ὑπηρέτης, a term the meaning of which has been much disputed, but which seems to imply some ministerial function higher than that of a mere attendant. After visiting Cyprus the little band proceeded to Perga in Pamphylia, where for some unknown reason Mark left his companions and returned to Jerusalem. The reticence of the Acts leaves us in doubt as to the motive of this desertion, but the most probable explanation is that he shrank from the difficulties and dangers of missionary work in the comparatively unknown country north of the Taurus. But whatever the reason of his conduct was S. Paul seems to have regarded it as blameworthy, since at the outset of the second journey he refused to allow him to accompany the party[4]. Hence arose a temporary alienation between S. Paul and S. Barnabas, and the latter sailed away to Cyprus, taking his cousin with him. From this time we hear nothing of S. Mark until incidental notices in two of S. Paul's Epistles of the first imprisonment show that he had been reconciled to the Apostle and was with him at Rome. S. Paul mentions him in the Epistle to Philemon in conjunction with Aristarchus,

---

[1] Col. iv. 10.　　　[2] Acts xii. 12.
[3] Acts xii. 25.　　　[4] Acts xv. 38.

Demas, and Luke; and commends him to the Colossians as one of his 'fellow-workers unto the kingdom of God,' who had proved a comfort to him [1]. Whether S. Mark ever carried out the intended visit to Colossae implied in the Epistle is not recorded; but that he did go to Asia is rendered probable by the fact that in the second Epistle to Timothy S. Paul begs his correspondent to bring Mark with him (presumably from Ephesus) to Rome [2].

One more most interesting allusion to the Evangelist occurs in the first Epistle of S. Peter, where the writer speaks of 'Mark my son [3].' The genuineness of the Epistle has been most vehemently denied by many critics, but the tendency of late years has been towards the removal of the doubts attaching to it [4]. The tone and contents of the letter make it probable that it was written from Rome, a supposition which is in harmony with the tradition recorded by Eusebius that the Babylon which it mentions is but a metaphorical name for the capital of the empire. An ingenious argument has been brought forward to show that this tradition rests ultimately on the authority of Papias. It may be noticed that in the passage from Eusebius quoted above the historian appeals both to Papias and to Clement. Now he elsewhere quotes Clement's words, which tell the same story as to the origin of the Gospel with this difference, that when the Apostle saw what was done he neither approved nor disapproved. It is probable therefore that the part of the tradition which does not rest on the testimony of Clement was derived from Papias. And since Eusebius also tells us that Papias quoted the first Epistle of S. Peter, the probability is great that what he did quote was the verse mentioning Babylon. If this be so we have high

---

[1] Philem. 24 ; Col. iv. 10.

[2] 2 Tim. iv. 11.

[3] 1 Pet. v. 13.

[4] Cf. Ramsay, *The Church in the Roman Empire*, c. xiii. V. *infra*. n. on p. 58.

authority both for the genuineness of the Epistle and for the connexion of the Gospel with Rome [1].

So far therefore from there being any difficulty in reconciling the New Testament notices of S. Mark with the traditional origin of the Gospel which bears his name, we may rather see in the John Mark of the Acts and Epistles a special fitness for the work which ancient authorities ascribe to him. As a native of Jerusalem, a man probably of good education and social position, a witness at any rate of the struggles and successes of the infant Church, and perhaps also of the crowning events of our Lord's life; the devoted follower of S. Paul, atoning for one youthful act of defection by years of faithful service in the cause of the Gospel; the disciple and companion of S. Peter, earning from him the affectionate title of son, S. Mark seems to have been a man peculiarly suited for the task of recording in a permanent form the facts which the Apostle set forth before his Roman hearers.

III. Evidence of the Gospel itself. Is it identical with the Gospel known to Papias? But we are now met by a far more difficult problem, that presented by the internal evidence of the Gospel itself. Is the Gospel of S. Mark which we know identical with that to which Papias refers? At first sight this question seems eminently unreasonable. Why should the existence of two Gospels be assumed, one of which must have been substituted for the other at an unknown date and without the slightest hint of the fact being anywhere recorded? Under modern literary conditions the idea would be absurd, and in face of the short interval which separates Papias from the Apostolic age, and of the fact that the Gospels must have been used in the public services of the Church, it is scarcely less unnatural to suppose that

---

[1] Cf. Salmon, *Introd. to N. T.*, Lect. XXII. Dr. Salmon concludes from the ὡς ἔφην in the fragment of Papias already quoted that he had previously alluded to the subject. It seems more natural, however, to refer the words simply to the ἑρμηνευτὴς Πέτρου γενόμενος in the preceding sentence.

a substitution of this kind can have taken place in the early days of Christianity. Indeed in this crude form the hypothesis has only been entertained by men who were determined beforehand to prove the untrustworthiness of the Gospels as historical records. And yet it contains an element of truth, or at any rate of possibility, which cannot be ignored. For it must be remembered that in ancient times a literary product had far less fixity than it has to-day. The functions of copyist and editor were not always clearly distinguished from each other, and, especially in Jewish circles, where the influence of oral tradition was paramount, transcribers would not scruple to alter, transpose, insert, and omit to a degree which a later age would have regarded as quite indefensible. To what extent this process could be carried is a much debated question, but it will be sufficient here to remark that we have no right to assume without proof the absolute identity of the text of S. Mark which we possess with that of the original Gospel as it left the hands of its author.

With this proviso therefore we may proceed to inquire whether there are any indications of date in the Gospel itself which would preclude the possibility of its traditional authorship. On this point there is a general agreement of opinion. No such indications can be found. None even of the so-called 'secondary features' of S. Mark—that is, the points (to be considered hereafter) in which S. Mark's narrative seems to show signs of posteriority to S. Matthew and S. Luke—necessitate a date so late that it could not be covered by the probable lifetime of the Evangelist.

But there are other considerations besides those of chronology. It is contended that the Gospel of S. Mark which we have can by no means be identical with the loose collection of anecdotes implied in the description of Papias. The order of the narrative in the canonical Gospel is clear: the Gospel which Papias knew possessed,

on his own showing, no order at all. The argument is
a plausible one, but a closer examination of the words
of Papias robs it of much of its force. Two points come
out very clearly in the fragment of that author preserved
by Eusebius. On the one hand he was firmly convinced
of S. Mark's accuracy, a fact which he emphasizes three
times, while at the same time he recognized and was
prepared to explain a want of order in the narrative.
Now although a man might conceivably insist on the
perfect accuracy of a loose collection of anecdotes, without considering whether the order of these anecdotes
corresponded with that of the events themselves, it is
quite as reasonable to suppose that Papias is here
defending the canonical Gospel from objections which
had been raised against it. Such objections might
naturally fall under two heads: (1) its incompleteness
as compared with the other Gospels; (2) differences in
the order of the narratives; and these two charges if
unanswered would go far towards weakening its authority.
The first gains some colour from the absence in S. Mark
of nearly all our Lord's great discourses, and a defender
of the Gospel would be quite likely to point to the fact
that the author had not been himself a follower of the
Saviour, and therefore was dependent on the testimony
of others for the events he describes, while his principal
informant never professed to have made a complete collection of these discourses, but only preserved such parts
of them as were suited to form the groundwork of his
own preaching. The second criticism would probably
be based on an unfavourable comparison of S. Mark
with one of the other Gospels. Which of them is the
most likely? In view of the fragmentary nature of the
extracts from Papias this question can only be con-
jecturally answered, and as a matter of fact each of the
three Gospels has had its advocates [1]. Perhaps on the

[1] For the list cf. Holtzmann, *Einleitung in das N.T.* p. 383 (third ed.).

whole, Dr. Salmon's suggestion[1] that S. Luke's order was regarded by Papias as the right one, has most to recommend it, although from the fact that S. Luke is not mentioned in any of the extant fragments of that author, it has found but few supporters. It certainly looks as if Papias were alluding to S. Luke's claim to write 'in order' (καθεξῆς) 'having traced the course of *all* things accurately from the first,' when he puts in a similar claim for the accuracy of S. Mark, allowing at the same time that the second Evangelist did not 'record *in order* (ἐν τάξει) what was said or done by Christ, but only wrote down *some things* as he remembered them.' And this view gains confirmation when a comparison between the two Gospels is made, starting from the point at which their narratives begin to run in parallel lines. In the very first chapter of S. Mark, as Dr. Salmon points out, the healing of S. Peter's wife's mother is placed after the call of the Apostle, while in S. Luke the order of the events is reversed[2]. In the third chapter the arrival of our Lord's mother and brethren to seek Him precedes the parable of the Sower: in S. Luke it follows it[3]. S. Mark relates the fact of the Baptist's imprisonment by Herod in connexion with the story of his death, and therefore out of its chronological order: S. Luke inserts it in its proper place[4]. S. Mark (like S. Matthew and S. John) records among the events of the Passion the anointing of our Lord in the house of Simon the leper: a very similar, if not the same, incident in the house of Simon the Pharisee is placed by S. Luke at the beginning of the ministry[5]. With regard to our Lord's sayings and discourses the differences are still more striking. The passages relating to Beelzebub and to the sin against the Holy Ghost,

---

[1] O. c., Lect. VII.
[2] Mark i. 30 ; Luke iv. 38.
[3] Mark iii. 31 f. ; Luke viii. 19 f.
[4] Mark vi. 17 f. ; Luke iii. 19, 20.
[5] Mark xiv. 3 f. ; Luke vii. 36 f.

which in S. Mark are closely connected, belong, according to S. Luke's narrative, to a later occasion and are separated from each other [1]. S. Mark makes our Lord inculcate the lesson of humility on His disciples in the course of the final journey up to Jerusalem; S. Luke introduces the words as spoken at the last supper [2]. And there are many more or less isolated sayings of our Lord, which are recorded by the two Evangelists in quite different contexts, as, for example, His words about the savour of salt [3], His answer to the question which was the first of the commandments [4], and His warning to the disciples to watch and pray in view of His second coming [5].

It is, of course, also the fact that there are considerable differences of order both between S. Mark and S. Matthew and between S. Mark and S. John; but in the first case the differences are not so numerous and striking as those of which examples have just been given [6], and in the second there is scarcely enough matter common to the two Gospels to render it probable that a comparison of this kind had been made between them.

But before the statements of Papias can be accepted as referring to the canonical Gospel of S. Mark, it is necessary to see whether that Gospel fulfils certain con-

[1] Mark iii. 22-30; Luke xi. 15-18; xii. 10.
[2] Mark x. 42-44; Luke xxii. 25, 26.
[3] Mark ix. 50; Luke xiv. 34.
[4] Mark xii. 28 f.; Luke x. 25-27.
[5] Mark xiii. 33; Luke xxi. 36.
[6] The principal differences between S. Matthew and S. Mark are (i) Our Lord's going to Capernaum is placed in S. Matthew before, in S. Mark after, the call of the four Apostles: Matt. iv. 13, Mark i. 21. (ii) In S. Matthew the healing of the leper follows the healing of S. Peter's wife's mother, in S. Mark it precedes it: Matt. viii. 2-4, Mark i. 40-45. (iii) The healing of the paralytic, the call of S. Matthew, the feast in his house, and the question of the Baptist's disciples, in S. Mark follow immediately the healing of the leper, in S. Matthew they are placed after the story of the Gadarene demoniac: Matt. ix. 1-17, Mark ii. 1-22. (iv) Two verses which occur in S. Matthew in the Sermon on the Mount have different contexts in S. Mark. Matt. v. 13 = Mark ix. 50; Matt. vi. 14 = Mark xi. 25.

ditions demanded by the hypothesis [1]. A work based immediately upon the personal recollections of one of the most prominent of the Apostles must bear about it some traces of its origin; it must show some of that minuteness and that vividness of detail which characterize the testimony of an eye-witness. Does the Gospel satisfy these conditions? In favour of an affirmative answer to this question there is a well-nigh universal agreement, for the number of minute particulars which S. Mark gives has been generally recognized as one of his distinctive peculiarities. 'There is perhaps not one narrative,' says Bishop Westcott, 'which he gives in common with S. Matthew and S. Luke, to which he does not contribute some special feature.' Without any attempt to give an exhaustive list of these special features, some of the most striking of them may be mentioned here. For instance, the Evangelist frequently records the effect of our Lord's words and acts on the minds of those who heard and saw them. When He came into 'His own country' and taught in the synagogue 'many hearing Him were astonished, saying, Whence hath this man these things [2]?' After the healing of the deaf and dumb man in Decapolis the witnesses of the miracle 'were beyond measure astonished, saying, He hath done all things well [3].' The disciples were 'astonished exceedingly' at our Lord's saying about the difficulty of a rich man entering the kingdom of God [4]. Especially does

(margin note: Indications that it is based on the testimony of an eye-witness.*)*

[1] The loss of Papias' *Expositions* makes it impossible to decide the question by reference to any quotations from the Gospel which he may have made. And even if it were discovered that these differed from the Marcan text, the general freedom of citation in early writers would prevent this from being conclusive evidence against the claims of the Gospel. It is perhaps worth mentioning that a chronicler of the ninth century, Georgius Hamartolus, refers to Papias as quoting Mark x. 38, 39, and that in this writer the quotation, with one slight difference (τὸ ποτήριόν μου for τὸ ποτήριον ὃ ἐγὼ πίνω), agrees verbally with the canonical text. The passage is quoted in Lightfoot's *Apostolic Fathers* (one volume edition) among the fragments of Papias.

[2] vi. 2.　　　[3] vii. 37.　　　[4] x. 26.

S. Mark bring out the slowness of the disciples to catch
the real meaning of our Lord's sayings and doings, their
inability to understand His predictions of His death and
resurrection, and their vague forebodings of evil as the
appointed time drew nigh. After the feeding of the
five thousand and the stilling of the waters 'they were
sore amazed in themselves; for they understood not
concerning the loaves, but their heart was hardened[1].'
They 'kept the saying' about His resurrection, 'ques-
tioning among themselves what the rising again from
the dead should mean[2].' In the final journey up to
Jerusalem 'Jesus was going before them and they were
amazed: and they that followed were afraid[3].' Passages
like these almost force upon us the conviction that they
embody the recollections of one who vividly recalls his
first impressions of scenes of which the true significance
was only brought home to him in the light of subsequent
events.

Again, in his description of incidents S. Mark frequently
adds minute details, which place the whole scene before
his readers with photographic clearness, and which are
often, while devoid of any apparent importance, just those
to imprint themselves indelibly on the memory of an
eye-witness. Zebedee left behind 'in the boat with the
hired servants,' when his two sons obeyed our Lord's
call[4]: the little boats accompanying the vessel into which
the waves beat while Jesus was asleep on the cushion[5]:
the five thousand sitting down 'in companies' (literally
garden-beds) upon the 'green grass[6]:' Bartimaeus casting
away his garment and springing up to meet his Bene-
factor[7]: our Lord Himself sitting down over against the
treasury and watching the multitude casting money into
it[8]; S. Peter among the officers in the court of the high
priest warming himself in the light of the fire[9]: such

[1] vi. 51, 52.   [2] ix. 10.   [3] x. 32.   [4] i. 20.   [5] iv. 36–38.
[6] vi. 39.   [7] x. 50.   [8] xii. 41.   [9] xiv. 54.

details as these are peculiarly characteristic of the second Gospel.

Further, with regard to the Person of the Redeemer Himself, S. Mark has preserved a number of particulars of infinite value. In six passages he records the original Aramaic words which our Lord used[1], and frequently refers to His feelings, His look, His gestures, thus hinting at the immediate motive of His acts. So we are told how Jesus, being moved with compassion, stretched forth His hand and touched the leper who had besought His aid[2]; how He looked round on the Pharisees with anger, being grieved at the hardening of their heart[3]; how He marvelled because of the unbelief of His own countrymen[4]; how when He saw a great multitude He had compassion on them, because they were as sheep not having a shepherd[5]; how He sighed deeply in His spirit, when He refused to satisfy the demand of the Pharisees for a sign[6]; how He took by the hand and raised up the boy possessed with the deaf and dumb spirit[7]; how He was moved with indignation at the disciples' rebuke of those who brought little children to Him, and how He took the children in His arms and laid His hands on them, and blessed them[8]. It is not unreasonable to conclude from such passages as these, that the Gospel of S. Mark is based on the testimony of one of our Lord's immediate disciples. Can we go further and say who that disciple was? Now the description of certain scenes at which only three witnesses were present—the raising of the daughter of Jairus[9], the Transfiguration[10], and the Agony in the garden[11]—at once raises the presumption that the Evangelist owes his knowledge of these events to one of the three. Of the disciples in question S. John is claimed as the author of an independent narrative, and the early martyrdom of

---

[1] iii. 17; v. 41; vii. 11, 34; xiv. 36; xv. 34.   [2] i. 41.
[3] iii. 5.   [4] vi. 6.   [5] vi. 34.   [6] viii. 12.   [7] ix. 27.   [8] x. 14 16.
[9] v. 35 f.   [10] ix. 2 f.   [11] xiv. 32 f.

S. James renders it (although not impossible) unlikely that the report emanated from him, so that the balance of evidence inclines in favour of S. Peter [1]. This conclusion is borne out especially by the record of the Transfiguration, which seems to contain the Apostle's own recollection of the half-unconscious words he had uttered as he gazed in bewilderment at the scene. It cannot be denied also that S. Peter does occupy a unique position in the Gospel [2]. It practically begins with the story of his call, followed by our Lord's visit to his house. The four disciples who formed the nucleus of the apostolic band are spoken of as 'Simon and they that were with him.' Obvious prominence is given to his confession 'Thou art the Christ,' to his rebuke of his Master when He foretold His rejection and death, and to his threefold denial. The authentic portion of the Gospel ends with the message sent to him by the angel at the tomb.

On the whole then we may claim that the contents of the second Gospel bear out the tradition of its Petrine origin. But before we leave this part of the subject one passage which presents a peculiar interest in relation to the question of authorship demands a separate consideration. Peculiar to S. Mark are the two verses [3] which tell the story of the young man clad in a linen cloth who

This eye-
witness
S. Peter.

S. Mark
relates one
experience
of his own.

[1] Cf. Salmon, *o. c.*, Lect. IX, where this point is well worked out.

[2] It must not be inferred from this that the second Gospel has, if we may use the expression, a monopoly of S. Peter. The other Gospels, as might be expected both from their superior length, and from the undoubted pre-eminence of S. Peter in the apostolic band, tell us some facts about the Apostle which are not mentioned in S. Mark. Cf. e. g. Matt. xiv. 29 f., xvi. 17, 18, xvii. 24, 25 ; Luke v. 8, xii. 41 ; John xiii. 6 f., xxi. 15 f. And there are three cases in which a saying or an act is definitely attributed to S. Peter in one of the other Gospels, while S. Mark simply refers it vaguely to 'the disciples' or 'to a certain one of them that stood by.' Matt. xv. 15 = Mark vii. 17 ; Luke viii. 45 = Mark v. 31 ; John xviii. 10 = Mark xiv. 47.

[3] xiv. 51, 52. For an interesting attempt to identify Gethsemane with the 'villa' (as the Vulgate translates χωρίον) of S. Mark himself, see an article in the *Expositor* for March, 1891. This would, at any rate, satisfactorily explain the mention of the 'linen cloth,' which was probably simply a sheet.

attempted to follow our Lord at the time of the betrayal at Gethsemane. The incident is apparently so trivial, so devoid of interest to any one except the person concerned, that it seems at first sight unworthy of its place in the history of the Passion. Moreover, there is the further difficulty of understanding who can have reported it, since the disciples had already forsaken their Master and fled. It is not surprising therefore that commentators of very different schools have agreed in accepting the only hypothesis which satisfactorily explains the motive of its insertion, namely, that it is an autobiographical detail, the young man being none other than S. Mark himself. Regarded from this point of view the episode at once gains a new and special significance. The one passage in the Gospel which betrays the personality of the author reveals also the fact that he was an eye-witness of the events which form the climax of his narrative.

PART II.

Relation to the other Synoptists.

HITHERTO we have been considering the Gospel of
S. Mark mainly as an isolated work. That is to say,
little or no account has been taken of the fact that side
by side with it in the New Testament are found two
other Gospels, so closely resembling it and each other in
matter and in form that the three have earned the name
of 'the Synoptists,' in contrast to the Gospel of S. John,
which stands alone and represents a different side of
evangelical tradition. The remarkable resemblances and
the not less remarkable differences between the Synoptic
Gospels make the question of their mutual relationship
an exceedingly intricate one, which is, however, of such
vital importance in connexion with the study of S. Mark
that it cannot be passed over.

What are the facts which a comparison of the three
Gospels brings to light? In the first place, there is, as
the name Synoptist implies, a general agreement between
the three as to plan: they give substantially the same
view of the same series of events. This agreement frequently extends further to the narration of a number of
incidents in the same order, and also in many cases to
verbal identity. It has been calculated that if the total
contents of the Synoptists be represented by 100, the
following table of peculiarities and coincidences is
obtained.

S. Mark has 7 peculiarities and 93 coincidences
S. Matthew 42 „ „ 58 „
S. Luke 59 „ „ 41 „

About two-fifths of the whole is common to all three
Gospels, while about one-third is peculiar to one or other

of them. S. Mark has (apart from the vivid details in which he abounds) not more than twenty-four verses of independent matter [1].

The verbal coincidences, although sufficiently striking, naturally do not extend so far as the coincidences of subject. They are most common in the case of our Lord's words and are comparatively rare in simple narrative. The examples of verbal agreement between S. Mark and S. Matthew are more numerous than those between S. Mark and S. Luke, but in the arrangement of events these two frequently coincide, where the first Gospel differs from them. Another interesting fact which was pointed out by one of the earliest of English modern critics, Bishop Marsh of Peterborough, is that in every instance where S. Matthew and S. Luke agree verbally in a section of which the matter is common to all three Gospels, S. Mark also agrees with them.

Such in bare outline are some of the most striking facts which form the basis of the Synoptic problem, although general statements can give but the most inadequate idea of that unity amid diversity and that diversity amid unity which must impress any one who has studied the three Gospels in relation to each other. How to account for these facts is one of the most important and most difficult questions of biblical criticism.

The Synoptic problem is essentially a modern one, dating in reality from the latter part of the eighteenth century. It seems surprising that the Christian world waited so long before approaching a question of such consummate importance, and yet an explanation of the fact is not difficult to find. In the first centuries of the Christian era men were comparatively little attracted by literary questions which depend for solution rather on internal analysis than on external testimony, and so the scantiness of historical tradition concerning the relations

[1] Cf. Westcott, *Introd. to Study of the Gospels*, c. iii.

of the Gospels to each other would account for the general
lack of interest in the subject. Again, at the Reformation
and post-Reformation periods the prevalence of a forced
and mechanical theory of inspiration acted as a deterrent.
There was a tendency to regard the very words of the
Bible as, so to speak, dictated by the Holy Spirit, a view
which made the Evangelists in effect the scribes and not
the authors of the works which bear their names. Hence
it was thought unnecessary, if not irreligious, to examine
the Gospels from a literary standpoint. At the present
day we have learnt by painful experience that criticism
is not incompatible with a belief in inspiration, but, at
least in the hands of Christian scholars presupposes, that
belief [1]. We feel now that, so far from being wrong, it
is the duty of biblical students to attempt to unravel
the problem of the origin of the Gospels by the aid
of the methods with which the increase of knowledge
and the growth of historical science has provided them.

Theories to account for these coincidences.

Broadly speaking we may divide Synoptic theories into
two main classes: those which base the Gospels immediately
on the oral tradition of the early Church, and those which
reject the oral theory as inadequate to explain the points
of agreement between the Gospels, and therefore suppose
either that the two later Evangelists copied from the
earlier one, whichever he may have been, or that all three
made use of some common document or documents which
have now perished.

(1) The oral hypothesis.

The hypothesis of oral tradition was first put forward
in detail by Gieseler in 1818 and up to the present time
has had many able advocates in England, while on the
Continent it has met with little favour. The theory rests
on the undeniable fact that the Jews at the time of Christ
were essentially a people of oral tradition. The Targums,
or paraphrases of the Old Testament, were transmitted
orally and it was forbidden to write them down. ' "Commit

---

[1] Cf. Driver, *Introd. to Literature of O. T.*, Preface, p. xx.

nothing to writing" was the characteristic principle of the earlier Rabbins, and even those who like Gamaliel were familiar with Greek learning faithfully observed it[1].'

Thus it came about that oral tradition among the Jews acquired a fixed and stereotyped character which we in modern times find it hard to realize. And since it may be assumed that in connexion with the synagogues intended for Greek-speaking Jews, like 'the synagogue of the Libertines, and of the Cyrenians, and of the Alexandrians[2],' a cycle of Greek as well as of Aramaic tradition would be formed, there is no *a priori* reason why the record of our Lord's life should not have been preserved in a similar manner. In fact there can be little doubt that for a considerable number of years it was so preserved. But the real question in relation to the Gospels is whether an oral tradition, however stereotyped, is enough by itself to account for the resemblances between the Synoptists.

It has been already remarked that these resemblances include coincidences in the events narrated, in the arrangement of those events, and in details of language. With regard to the first two classes it is clear that we must assume a peculiar fixity in the oral tradition if it is to account both for the identity of the incidents and for the identity of their order. But even supposing that this assumption were a justifiable one, there would remain another and a more serious difficulty behind. Where did this cycle of tradition grow up? If, as is generally supposed, at Jerusalem, why is our Lord's Judaean ministry only so obscurely hinted at in the Synoptists[3]? The difficulty of accounting for the differences between the Synoptists and the fourth Gospel is most seriously enhanced on the oral hypothesis, since at Jerusalem the

[margin note: This rejected as inadequate.]

---

[1] Westcott, *o. c.*, c. iii. p. 167.
[2] Acts vi. 9.
[3] Cf. Dr. Sanday's 'Survey of the Synoptic Question,' in the *Expositor*, Feb.-June, 1891 (esp. Paper II.).

influence of S. John must have been very great, and he
would certainly have contributed largely to the formation
of a body of tradition which accumulated there.   The
omissions in the Synoptists make it almost incredible that
their narratives can represent a central tradition which
emanated from the mother Church.

Again, it is equally difficult to account for the coincidences in language, since these extend beyond the record
of our Lord's words, where we should expect to find them,
to passages of pure narrative, and even to connecting
phrases which would be the first to fall out or be changed
in an oral Gospel.   For instance, in the account of the call
of S. Peter and S. Andrew the parenthetical statement 'for
they were fishers' is found both in S. Matthew and S.
Mark[1].   A still more striking example of the same kind
occurs in the story of the healing of the paralytic at
Capernaum, in which all three Evangelists insert into the
middle of our Lord's own words the parenthesis 'He saith
to the sick of the palsy[2].'   The three agree again in having
the same phrase 'and they laughed Him to scorn' in their
report of the raising of Jairus' daughter[3].   S. Matthew
and S. Mark both end their account of the last supper
with the notice, 'And when they had sung a hymn
they went out unto the mount of Olives[4].'   In the
narrative of the betrayal all three Gospels insert the
apparently superfluous reminder that Judas was 'one of
the twelve[5].'

The frequent recurrence of points like these seems to
show that a body of oral tradition cannot be the main
factor in the composition of the triple Synopsis.   On the

---

[1] Matt. iv. 18; Mark i. 16.

[2] Matt. ix. 6; Mark ii. 10; Luke v. 24.   There are slight verbal differences in the parenthesis.   S. Matthew has τότε λέγει τῷ παραλιτικῷ.
S. Mark omits τότε; S. Luke has εἶπε τῷ παραλελυμένῳ.

[3] Matt. ix. 24; Mark v. 40; Luke viii. 53.

[4] Matt. xxvi. 30; Mark xiv. 26.

[5] Matt. xxvi. 47; Mark xiv. 43; Luke xxii. 47.

other hand we are not justified in ignoring its existence so
entirely as many critics, especially in Germany, have done.
For after all there must have been many floating traditions
about our Lord's life current in the early Church, and it
would be strange if the Evangelists had been entirely
uninfluenced by these. To what extent, however, we may
introduce the oral hypothesis to supplement other theories
is a difficult question the discussion of which may be for
the present deferred.

If the oral theory be rejected as inadequate, we are (2) Other
driven to conclude either that the Evangelists copied one theories.
from another, or that they all made use of a common
written source. In the first case, it is clear that there is
room for six different theories according to the order in
which the Gospels are supposed to have been written.
The field, however, is considerably narrowed by the number
and extent of the differences in matter between S. Matthew
and S. Luke, differences which make it incredible that
either Evangelist can have made the work of the other
the basis of his own Gospel, although they might conceivably be compatible with an occasional and subsidiary
influence of one on the other. Practically therefore all
we have to consider is the relation of S. Mark to these
two Gospels, and so we are brought face to face with the
question, Is S. Mark the latest or the earliest of the three?
Is it an abridged combination of S. Matthew and S. Luke,
or the common source to which each of the later Evangelists has added independent matter of his own? The former (a) S. Mark
hypothesis, which is connected mainly with the name of an abridge-
ment of S.
Griesbach, received a certain amount of support from the Matthew
and S.
saying of S. Augustine that S. Mark was the follower and Luke.
abridger of S. Matthew, but was based chiefly on the
evidence of a few passages in which the second Gospel
appeared to combine the accounts of the first and third.
A good example of the passages in question is Mark i. 32,
where it was maintained that the phrase 'at even when

the sun did set' was a combination of S. Matthew's 'when even was come,' and S. Luke's 'when the sun was setting[1].' It is obvious, however, that a phenomenon of this kind is equally explicable on the supposition that the double phrase is the earlier form, and that S. Matthew and S. Luke have each preserved one-half of it, dropping the other half as superfluous.

This 'combination theory' derived a fictitious importance from the fact that it was adopted (although on other grounds) by the Tübingen school of criticism. The historical theory of Baur that the early Church was split into two fiercely contending factions, the Ebionite or Judaistic, and the Pauline, and that out of the ruins of their disputes arose in the middle of the second century the fabric of Catholic Christianity, compelled him to push down the dates of the Gospels as late as possible, and as S. Mark shows no traces of the supposed quarrels it was relegated as a 'neutral' document to about the year 170, when the process of reconciliation was supposed to have been completed. No one could attribute so late a date to S. Mark unless he were, as Aristotle says, ' maintaining a thesis,' and in this extreme position Baur has been followed by few even of his own disciples.

Contrary indications of priority in S. Mark. But quite apart from its Tübingen developments there are serious objections against Griesbach's hypothesis.

In the first place, if the second Evangelist was acquainted with the Gospels of S. Matthew and S. Luke, it is impossible to imagine what motive can have induced him to omit so many things which they record. That a shorter Gospel may have been expanded into two longer ones is quite a credible supposition ; the reverse process is always inconceivable.

Again, the multiplicity of vivid details, which, as has been already pointed out, is one of the most striking characteristics of S. Mark's Gospel, is utterly incompatible

[1] Matt. viii. 16; Luke iv. 40.

with the theory that it is a late compilation from two earlier works. It is true, of course, that abundance of detail is not always a criterion of early date. But the kind of matter which a writer living long after the events he describes adds in order to atone by his historical imagination for his want of real knowledge, is as different as possible from the minute, unobtrusive touches, which lend such a unique interest to S. Mark's narrative. One only needs to place S. Mark side by side with any of the apocryphal Gospels to feel at once the impassable gulf which divides the two.

Thirdly, the theory fails to account for the absence in S. Mark of a number of words and phrases which are of frequent occurrence in the other Synoptists [1].

Another indication of the priority of S. Mark is his use of expressions which are condemned by grammarians as colloquial and vulgar [2]. These expressions are for the

---

[1] Cf Holtzmann. *o. c.*, p. 354. The following are some of the expressions not found in S. Mark (or found only in the last twelve verses) which are characteristic of the other Gospels :—

(a) S. Matthew. ὥσπερ, ὕστερον. ἄρτι, ἐν ἐκείνῳ τῷ καιρῷ, παρουσία, ὁ λόγος (τὸ εὐαγγέλιον) τῆς βασιλείας, ἡ βασιλεία τῶν οὐρανῶν, φαίνεσθαι (in the sense of ʻto be manifestedʼ), δικαιοσύνη, συμφέρειν (intransitive), ἐρρέθην.

(b) S. Luke. μετὰ ταῦτα, παραχρῆμα, ἐπιστάτης, ὁ κύριος (of Christ), χάρις. χωρίζεσθαι, σωτήρ, σωτηρία, ἐφιστάναι, ὑποστρέφειν, ὑπάρχειν, ἀδικία, ἐνώπιον, εὐαγγελίζεσθαι, προσδοκᾶν.

(c) Both S. Matthew and S. Luke. οὗ, νόμος, ἄξιος, ἕτερος, ἀμφότεροι, δικαιοῦν, ἁμαρτάνειν, κρίνειν, κρύπτειν, καθιστάναι, ἀποκαλύπτειν, ἐργάτης, μακάριος.

[2] Cf. Abbott, *Encycl. Brit.*, art. ʻGospels.ʼ

In the account of the healing of the paralytic in c. ii., S. Mark four times uses the word κράββατος for bed, while S. Matthew has κλίνη, and S. Luke κλίνη, κλινίδιον, or the paraphrase ἐφ᾽ ὃ κατέκειτο. The grammarian Phrynichus says σκίμπους λέγε, ἀλλὰ μὴ κράββατος.

Mark v. 23 τὸ θυγάτριόν μου ἐσχάτως ἔχει. Matt. ix. 18 ἄρτι ἐτελεύτησεν. Luke viii. 42 ἀπέθνησκεν. Phrynichus ἐσχάτως ἔχει ἐπὶ τοῦ μοχθηρῶς ἔχει καὶ σφαλερῶς τάττουσιν οἱ σύρφακες.

Mark xiv. 65 ῥαπίσμασιν ἔλαβον. S. Matthew avoids the substantive, but uses the verb ῥαπίζειν (xxvi. 68 , while S. Luke has παίειν (xxii. 64 ; Phrynichus τὸ ῥάπισμα οὐκ ἐν χρήσει· χρῶ οὖν τῷ κρείττονι. τὸ γὰρ τὴν γνάθον πλατείᾳ τῇ χειρὶ πλῆξαι, ἐπὶ κόρρης πατάξαι Ἀθηναῖοι φασίν.

Mark xv. 43 εὐσχήμων βουλευτής. Matt. xxvii. 57 ἄνθρωπος πλούσιος. Luke xxiv. 50 βουλευτὴς ὑπάρχων, ἀνὴρ ἀγαθὸς καὶ δίκαιος. Phrynichus τοῦτο μὲν εὐσχήμων) οἱ ἀμαθεῖς ἐπὶ τοῦ πλουσίου καὶ ἐν ἀξιώματι ὄντος τάττουσιν· οἱ δὲ ἀρχαῖοι ἐπὶ τοῦ καλοῦ καὶ συμμέτρου.

most part absent in the parallel passages of S. Matthew and S. Luke, and it is extremely unlikely that a late Gospel would exhibit a retrogression of this kind in point of style.

Again, the second Gospel contains many expressions which might be stumbling-blocks in the way of weak believers, as seeming either to show a want of reverence for the Lord, or to place a limit to His supernatural powers, or again to reflect on the characters of the disciples. Such expressions constitute a strong proof of the antiquity of the Gospel in which they occur, especially when we find them omitted or modified in the other Gospels. For instance—

Mark i. 34. 'And He healed *many* that were sick with divers diseases.' S. Matthew tell us that He 'healed *all* that were sick,' and S. Luke that He 'laid his hands *on every one* of them and healed them [1].'

Mark iii. 21. 'And when His friends heard it, they went out to lay hold on Him : for they said, He is beside Himself.' This is altogether omitted by both the other Evangelists.

Mark vi. 3. 'Is not this the carpenter ?' S. Matthew has 'the carpenter's son [2].'

Mark vi. 5, 6. 'And He could there do no mighty work, save that He laid His hands upon a few sick folk and healed them. And He marvelled because of their unbelief.' S. Matthew simply says, 'And He did not many mighty works there because of their unbelief [3].'

Mark vi. 51, 52. 'And they were sore amazed in themselves ; for they understood not concerning the loaves, but their heart was hardened.' This is entirely omitted in the parallel narrative of S. Matthew, who inserts instead, 'And they that were in the boat worshipped Him, saying, Of a truth Thou art the Son of God [4].'

Mark x. 35. S. Mark makes the request that S. James

---

[1] Matt. viii. 16 ; Luke iv. 40.   [2] Matt. xiii. 55 ; cf. Luke iv. 22.
[3] Matt. xiii. 58.   [4] Matt. xiv. 33.

and S. John might share our Lord's glory proceed from the two disciples themselves, while S. Matthew's account seems to attribute it to the ambition of their mother [1].

From the foregoing considerations it seems a fair conclusion that the 'combination' theory is untenable, and so by a process of exhaustion we are brought to the necessity of deciding between the two remaining hypotheses, the one being that the second Gospel was used by the writers of the first and third, the other that behind all three lies a common document which has perished. In other words, the question is whether the common basis of the triple Synopsis is the canonical S. Mark, or a still earlier document on which that Gospel is itself founded [2]. The possibility that the original S. Mark was not identical with our Gospel has been already mentioned in connexion with the statements of Papias, and the conclusion was drawn that as far as the Gospel itself was concerned, there were no indications in it of a date inconsistent with its traditional authorship. We have now to ask whether a comparison of S. Mark with the other Synoptists confirms that view or not. What does an examination of S. Matthew and S. Luke tell us about the nature of the source or sources from which their common matter is taken ?

v. S. Matthew and S. Luke expansions of either S. Mark or a document most nearly represented by it.

Here the problem becomes complicated by the fact that the agreement of these two Gospels goes a good way beyond the limits covered by the second Gospel ; and so the question arises whether this additional matter was originally included in the Marcan tradition, and for some reason or other had fallen out by the time the tradition became fixed in its present form, or whether it can be accounted for in some other way.

One of the peculiar difficulties of the Synoptic problem lies in the close connexion existing between its various

[1] Matt. xx. 20.
[2] For the sake of convenience, this supposed document will be referred to as the 'Urmarcus,' or original Mark, which is the name given to it in Germany.

parts. The decision arrived at on any one point almost necessarily affects the view taken of the whole. And the question just raised constitutes no exception to the general rule. Nevertheless we must for the moment leave it unanswered and confine our attention to the triple Synopsis; that is, to the matter which S. Matthew and S. Luke have in common with S. Mark.

This document coincident in order with S. Mark. In the second volume of *Studia Biblica* Mr. F. H. Woods has by a process of skilful reasoning elucidated a fact which has of late years been generally, but in most cases only vaguely, recognized, namely, that (to quote his own words) 'the original basis of the Synoptical Gospels coincided in its range and order with our S. Mark [1].' He grounds this conclusion on the following observations: (a) The earliest and latest parallels in all three Gospels coincide with the beginning and end of S. Mark. The first is the ministry of S. John the Baptist, the last the visit of the women to our Saviour's tomb. (b) With but few exceptions we find parallels to the whole of S. Mark in either S. Matthew or S. Luke and to by far the larger part in both. (c) The order of the whole of S. Mark, excepting of course what is peculiar to that Gospel, is confirmed either by S. Matthew or S. Luke, and the greater part of it by both. (d) A passage parallel in all three Synoptists is never immediately followed in both S. Matthew and S. Luke by a separate incident common to these two Evangelists alone. (e) Similarly, in the parts common to S. Matthew and S. Luke alone, no considerable fragments, with some doubtful exceptions, occur in the same relative order, so that it is unlikely that they formed part of the original source. (f) To this we may add the fact that in these parts the differences between S. Matthew and S. Luke are generally greater than in those which are common to all three.

---

[1] i.e. excluding the last twelve verses, against the genuineness of which, as will be seen below, there is strong evidence.

It is undeniable that if those facts can be established, the evidence which they present is extraordinarily strong, and no one who has followed out in detail Mr. Woods' reasoning can fail to be convinced that in its main outlines at least he has proved his case. It is of course impossible within the limits of this essay to do more than show by a few examples the method by which he has arrived at his conclusions.

Dividing S. Mark for the sake of convenience into three parts, (A) i-iii. 6; (B) iii. 7-vi. 13; (C) vi. 14-xvi. 8, he shows that in (A) the order of S. Mark exactly agrees with that of S. Luke and mainly with that of S. Matthew; in (B) the order agrees with either S. Matthew or S. Luke and in parts with both; in (C) the order agrees exactly with S. Matthew and mainly with S. Luke. It is especially noticeable that the parallelisms continually overlap one another; for instance, in (A) the parallelism with S. Luke overlaps a new parallelism with S. Matthew, which begins with Matt. xii. 1 = Mark ii. 23 and continues to a point in the middle of (B) Matt. xiii. 34 = Mark iv. 34 a. This is a proof that the source on which S. Matthew and S. Luke drew was a whole Gospel in the Marcan order, and not a number of independent documents which were afterwards pieced together to form S. Mark's Gospel. That this general identity of order is not more obvious is due mainly to three causes. In the first place, both S. Matthew and S. Luke interpolated into the Marcan tradition a large amount of matter from other sources. Secondly, these additions contain much that is identical with or very similar to things recorded in S. Mark. Thirdly, where this is the case both Evangelists frequently omit the corresponding Marcan passages [1]. As examples of the first

[1] These considerations will also explain the apparent discrepancy between the argument here and the illustrations of the differences in order between S. Mark and S. Luke which were given on pp. 17 and 18 in connexion with the sayings of Papias. It must also be borne in mind that differences in language and detail make it most probable that in

cause of confusion it is sufficient to point to the dislocation
produced by the insertion of the Sermon on the Mount in
S. Matthew and of the ' Sermon on the Plain ' and the
great Peraean section in S. Luke, while a comparison of
the fourth chapter of S. Mark with the corresponding
thirteenth chapter of S. Matthew will serve to illustrate
the extent to which the later Evangelist allowed himself
to deviate from the order of the Marcan tradition. In the
first two paragraphs (Mark vv. 1–20 ; Matt. vv. 1–23), con-
taining the parable of the Sower and its explanation, the
two Gospels run parallel with each other, with the exception of the fact that S. Matthew, besides adding a verse
or two peculiar to himself, has taken v. 25 of S. Mark
and inserted it as v. 12 in what is perhaps a more
suitable context. Then come four verses of S. Mark,
21–24 inclusive, which are omitted in S. Matthew, 21 and
24 because they had already occurred in the Sermon on
the Mount [1], 22 and 23 because they are found in a section
of S. Matthew (x. 15–xi. 30) which is probably not taken
from the Marcan tradition [2]. Verse 25 has just been
accounted for. In place of 26–29, the parable of the seed
growing secretly, we have the more striking parable of the
tares; 30–35 correspond to 31–36 of S. Matthew, who has
here also added some matter of his own. The event
recorded in 35–41 is omitted here, because S. Matthew has
already related it in ch. viii., which forms part of a section
(viii–x. 14) of his Gospel, in which he has incorporated
a number of passages from S. Mark out of their proper
order, being influenced, as Mr. Woods says, partly ' by the

S. Luke many of the seeming parallels to S. Mark were taken from a
non-Marcan source. This is the case especially with the call of S. Peter
(Luke v. 1–11) and the anointing in the house of Simon (Luke vii. 36–50).

[1] v. 15 ; vii. 2.

[2] Because, with the exception of x. 17–22 and 42, there are no parallels
to this section in S. Mark, and the passage x. 17–22 is a doublet, i.e. it
occurs again in its proper Marcan context (Matt. xxiv. 9–14 = Mark xiii.
9–13 , which seems to imply that in this context it is taken from a
different source.

desire to group the miracles together, but partly also by
the order and contents of the Marcan tradition upon which
his Gospel was based [1].'

The section chosen for comparison probably conveys an
exaggerated impression of the amount of difference in
order between S. Mark and S. Matthew, and might not
unreasonably give rise to the suspicion that a theory
which has to postulate so many omissions, transpositions,
and borrowings from other sources in order to explain the
phenomena it deals with, is too complicated and ingenious
to be true.

To allay this suspicion two considerations may be
put forward. In the first place, the normal amount of
deviation in order is not nearly so great as might be
imagined from this chapter alone; and secondly, where
S. Matthew has deviated from the Marcan order in this
chapter, S. Luke in the corresponding chapter of his
Gospel (ch. viii.) has preserved it. Similarly both in
this chapter and elsewhere it has been found that where
S. Luke deviates S. Matthew keeps faithfully to his
original.

Thus we seem to be justified in concluding that the
matter common to the Synoptists was derived from a
document identical in order with our S. Mark. From this,
however, it does not inevitably follow that the Gospel of
S. Mark is exactly coextensive with the Marcan tradition.
And so it is necessary to face the question of possible
additions or omissions in the canonical Gospel, a question
which a few pages back was raised but left undiscussed.

Was it also identical in range?

The number of possible additions is comparatively small,
since there-is so little in S. Mark to which no parallel
occurs either in S. Matthew or in S. Luke. But besides the
minute details characteristic of S. Mark, there are also
a few passages peculiar to him, which deserve separate
mention.

[1] *O. c.* p. 71.

(*a*) i. 1 and 2 b.   It has been thought that the first verse of the Gospel is a later addition, but the reasons for this view are not very obvious, unless like some critics we hold that a Gospel without an end ought also to be a Gospel without a beginning.   The simple exordium is quite in character with the style of S. Mark, and would naturally be omitted by the later Evangelists.   As ·regards 2 b the fact that it is ascribed to Isaiah instead of to Malachi, and also that it is quoted in another connexion by both S. Matthew and S. Luke[1], is quite enough to account for its omission here.

(*b*) iv. 26–29.   The omission by S. Matthew of the parable of the seed growing secretly has been already noticed and accounted for by his insertion of the similar but more striking parable of the tares. The fact that S. Luke also omits it may be due partly to his rearrangement of Marcan matter, partly to its general similarity to the parables of the sower and the mustard-seed.   The third Evangelist seems intentionally to avoid recording two similar incidents or sayings.

(*c*) vii. 2–4 is probably omitted by S. Matthew as unnecessary for his Jewish readers.

(*d*) vii. 32–37.   For this S. Matthew substitutes a general statement about our Lord's miracles of healing (xv. 30–31).

(*e*) viii. 22–26 seems omitted by S. Matthew because of the similar miracle which he records in ix. 27–31[2].

(*f*) xii. 32–34 a.   Mr. Woods suggests that this was omitted by S. Matthew because the words of the lawyer and what immediately followed were 'partly in a certain sense a repetition of our Lord's own language, and partly a merely personal incident.'

(*g*) xiv. 51–52.   This incident, as has been already noted, might easily fall out of the later Gospels, since it appeared to have no interest for any one except the man concerned.

(*h*) ix. 48, 49, 50 b ; xi. 25.   In addition to these passages there are some verses which seem out of place in their contexts and may possibly be marginal notes which have crept into the text.   It is curious that in both passages some manuscripts have additions which are undoubtedly of this description[3].   On the other hand, it is equally possible, and perhaps on the whole more probable, that these verses are isolated sayings of our Lord which S. Mark wished to incorporate in his Gospel, and so inserted in discourses with the subjects of which they were more or less closely connected, although they were not originally spoken at the same time.   If this be the case, it is quite

[1] Matt. xi. 10 ; Luke vii. 27.

[2] It is noticeable that *c*, *d*, and *e* occur in the section of the Gospel (vi. 45–viii. 26) which is wholly omitted by S. Luke, so that no inference can be drawn from a comparison with the third Gospel.

[3] To ix. 49 'Western' authorities add, 'And every sacrifice shall be salted with salt,' and to xi. 26, 'But if ye do not forgive, neither will your Father which is in heaven forgive your trespasses.'

natural that S. Matthew, with his love for grouping and arranging our
Lord's sayings, should omit the verses.

(*i*) xvi. 9–20. There remains to be considered one passage which The last
stands on a footing quite different from that of any of the other twelve
possible additions to the original Gospel. This is xvi. 9–20, the verses
genuineness of which has been a disputed point from at least the part of the
time of Eusebius onwards. There is now a fairly general agreement Marcan
that these twelve verses did not form part of the original Marcan tradition.
tradition. The evidence against them is strong and of various kinds.
They are omitted in the two oldest uncial manuscripts, the Sinaitic
and the Vatican, and although the force of this conjoint testimony is
somewhat weakened by the fact that the leaf of the Sinaitic codex on
which the Gospel ends is one of six which were probably written by
the scribe of the Vatican, yet the witness of even one of such manuscripts cannot be lightly set aside. Besides these, two other later
uncials, L (Regius) and Ψ (Athous), cast doubt on the genuineness of
the verses by adding an alternative shorter conclusion. A few manuscripts of versions omit them, such as *k* of the Old Latin, some of the
best Armenian, and, most important of all, the newly discovered
Sinaitic palimpsest of the Syriac Gospels. Eusebius, who tells us
that the 'accurate copies' of the Gospel end with ver. 8, seems to
decide, though with hesitation, against the verses. The commentator
Victor of Antioch does not go beyond ver. 8, and there are no
references to the succeeding verses in writers who would have been
most likely to quote from them, notably Cyril of Jerusalem, Tertullian, and Cyprian.

Besides this external testimony there are objections arising out of
the style and contents of the section itself. It lacks literary con-
tinuity with what precedes it. The phrase 'early on the first day
of the week' (πρωὶ πρώτῃ σαββάτου) is unnecessary and awkward after
the 'very early on the first day of the week' (λίαν πρωὶ τῇ μιᾷ τῶν
σαββάτων) of verse 2. Again, Mary Magdalene seems to be introduced
to the reader as though she had not been mentioned before, whereas
her name has already appeared once in the same chapter and twice
in the preceding. Further, there are in the section an unusual
number of words and phrases which do not occur elsewhere in the
Gospel [1]. The presence of these would not be sufficient by itself to
prove a difference of authorship, but they have appreciable force in
confirming suspicions which have been raised on other grounds. But
more striking than any of the above-mentioned facts is the cessation

---

[1] The following is a list of these words and phrases:—φαίνεσθαι (in the
sense of 'to be manifested'), φανεροῦσθαι (in the same sense, three times),
πορεύεσθαι (three times), θεᾶσθαι (twice), ἀπιστεῖν (twice, πενθεῖν, παρακο-
λουθεῖν, ἐπακολουθεῖν, βεβαιοῦν, ἀναλαμβάνειν, συνεργεῖν, ἐκεῖνος (emphatic,
twice), ἕτερος, ὕστερον, θανάσιμος, μετὰ ταῦτα, μὲν οὖν. Besides these there
is found ὁ Κύριος, which never occurs as a title of our Lord in the narrative
portions of S. Mark.

of the parallelism between S. Matthew and S. Luke at the point corresponding to verse 8[1].

The extreme improbability that both Evangelists would have so far departed from their usual custom as to ignore a section of such importance is a strong proof that it was known to neither of them.

Thus various kinds of evidence converge to prove that the concluding verses are not contemporaneous with the rest of the Gospel. But there is no indication that any part of the canonical S. Mark, with the exception of this section, was not included in the original Marcan tradition.

It is necessary now to inquire whether this original tradition itself included anything which in the canonical Gospel has been omitted.

Supposed omissions in the Gospel. It has been already observed that the agreement between S. Matthew and S. Luke extends a considerable way beyond the matter common to them with S. Mark. In the account of the Baptist's preaching, of the Temptation, in parts of the Sermon on the Mount and of other discourses, we find a general parallelism of matter which occasionally passes into identity of language. Did this common matter exist in the original Marcan tradition and fall out before the Gospel reached its present form, or was it taken from some other source or sources? It is clear that the mere fact of the inclusion of a passage in S. Matthew and S. Luke is no proof that it was derived from the Marcan tradition, unless it stands in the two Gospels in a parallel sequence of narrative which goes backwards or forwards to a point where both agree with S. Mark. But although this principle excludes many passages which might otherwise claim a Marcan origin, yet there are a certain number which are unaffected by it. It will be best therefore to examine these passages in order.

(*a*) Matt. iii. 7-10; Luke iii. 7-9, 17. The preaching of the Baptist. Here the agreement between S. Matthew and S. Luke is exceedingly close both in matter and language, and the context in all three Gospels both before and after agrees but for the verses peculiar to S. Luke (5, 6, 10-15, 18-20). The parallelism is so remarkable that it has led Mr. Woods to think that S. Mark has omitted some verses from the original source, possibly as not being suited to his Gentile

---

[1] Matt. xxviii. 8; Luke xxiv. 10.

readers. This is of course quite possible, but it is not a necessary hypothesis. And S. Luke's words in verse 18, 'With many other exhortations therefore preached he good tidings unto the people' suggest the idea that he was making selections from the Baptist's discourses, and might have reported them at greater length had he been so disposed. If this be the case, the source from which he was drawing is not so likely to have been the Marcan tradition, which gives but a brief and compressed account of all events preceding the call of S. Peter, as some independent record of the Baptist's preaching. Again, it is curious that the verses under discussion contain (besides several rare words, which prove nothing) some words not uncommon in the New Testament, but which are not found in S. Mark [1]. However, an argument of this kind is always precarious, especially in a case where the words of a speaker are being reported, so that no stress can be laid on it here. Still on the whole the available evidence seems to favour the hypothesis that both the later Evangelists supplemented the Marcan report from another source, from which S. Luke has quoted most fully. The close agreement in language between the two Evangelists suggests that this source was a written and not an oral one.

(*b*) The Temptation. Mark i. 12, 13; Matt. iv. 1-11; Luke iv. 1-13. At first sight the extreme brevity of S. Mark's account of the Temptation creates the impression that he has merely abridged the fuller narratives of the two other Evangelists, omitting the mention of the fasting and all the details of the three temptations. And yet his version possesses certain peculiar features which seem incompatible with this view. According to him the temptation appears to have been continuous, as also was the ministry of angels. He alone mentions the wild beasts. Again, it is far more probable that the phrase 'the Spirit driveth him forth into the wilderness' should have been changed to 'Then was Jesus led up of the Spirit into the wilderness' and 'was led by the Spirit in the wilderness,' than that either of these should have given place to the stronger but more mysterious expression of S. Mark. Moreover, it is difficult to understand why the record of the three specific temptations should have dropped out : no satisfactory reason for the supposed omission seems ever to have been suggested.

(*c*) The Sermon on the Mount. Matt. v. 1-vii. 28; Luke vi. 20-49. It has been supposed, although there appears to be now a general tendency to abandon the idea, that the Sermon on the Mount formed a part of the original Gospel. But the difficulties in the way of this supposition are very serious. In the first place, while all three Gospels relate the gathering round our Lord of multitudes who came from widely different quarters, S. Mark distinctly says that the reason of their coming was the widespread fame of His powers of

---

[1] ὑποδεικνύναι, ἐκκόπτειν, κεῖσθαι, ἄξιος, καρπὸν 'καρποὺς' ποιεῖν, καρπός does not occur in S. Mark, except in the literal sense.

healing, and gives no hint of the fact that they were desirous to hear Him speak. Again, His withdrawal from the crowd into a ship, an incident which the other Gospels omit, seems to negative the idea that according to S. Mark He had any intention of delivering a discourse. It is therefore most natural to suppose that S. Matthew and S. Luke both saw in this passage of S. Mark a suitable occasion for the insertion of the Sermon, the report of which they got from other sources, and that each in his own way slightly modified the language of S. Mark in order to lead up to it. It may be added that the differences between the two versions of the Sermon are far greater than is usually the case in places where the two later Evangelists are both using S. Mark, if indeed they are compatible with the use of a common document at all. The occurrence also of two sayings out of the Sermon in other contexts in S. Mark is another fact of some significance [1].

If the Sermon was derived from a source other than the Marcan tradition, it naturally follows that the healing of the centurion's servant, which is closely connected with it both in S. Matthew and S. Luke, was also not part of the tradition.

(*d*) The Beelzebub Discourse. Matt. xii.; Mark iii.; Luke xi. Here the agreement in matter between S. Matthew and S. Luke extends some way beyond S. Mark's account, which does not contain parallels to vv. 27, 28, 30, of S. Matthew = vv. 19, 20, 23, of S. Luke.

It must be observed in the first place that the Lucan parallel occurs in the great central section of the Gospel which takes the place of Mark ix. 41–x. 12, and which, although it contains some parallels to S. Mark, was almost certainly not taken from the Marcan tradition [2]. Secondly, the agreement in language between S. Luke and S. Matthew is much closer than that between S. Luke and S. Mark, a state of things which is very unusual. It is probable therefore that both S. Matthew and S. Luke derived their reports from a non-Marcan source, and that S. Matthew substituted this version in place of the less complete account of S. Mark.

(*e*) The Missionary Discourses. Matt. x.; Mark vi. 7–11; Luke ix. 1–11, x. 1–16. In this case the question is complicated by the existence in S. Luke of two very similar discourses, one addressed to the twelve and the other to the seventy, and both showing affinities in different ways to the single accounts of S. Matthew and S. Mark. The first agrees very closely with S. Mark, the second adds considerably to it, most of the additional matter being found also in S. Matthew. The fact that the second discourse in S. Luke occurs in the central section makes it improbable that the additional matter in it was derived from a Marcan source, and so the most natural explanation of the facts of the case is that S. Luke borrowed his first discourse directly from S. Mark, and that for the second he was

[1] Matt. v. 13 = Mark ix. 50 (cf. Luke xiv. 34). Matt. vii. 2 = Mark iv. 24, Luke vi. 38.
[2] See Mr. Wood's exhaustive proof of this. *O. c.* pp. 77–79.

indebted to some other source, which was also made use of by S. Matthew.

(*f*) The Parable of the Leaven. Matt. xiii. 33; Luke xiii. 21. This parable may have been omitted in S. Mark, but the fact that S. Luke's version is found in the central section of the Gospel and that his language in the preceding parable of the mustard-seed resembles S. Matthew's more closely than S. Mark's makes it probable that both S. Matthew and S. Luke took it from a non-Marcan source.

(*g*) Matt. xviii. 7; Luke xvii. 1. This verse also occurs in the central section of S. Luke, and moreover the difference in language between the two versions of the saying is greater than is usually the case when both Evangelists are following S. Mark.

(*h*) The Eschatological Discourses. Matt. xxiv., xxv.; Mark xiii.; Luke xxi. 5-36; cf. xii. 35-48 and xvii. 2c-37. The case of these discourses closely resembles that of the missionary discourses, but forms perhaps a still more complicated problem. Matt. xxiv. 1-36. Mark xiii. 1-32, and Luke xxi. 5-35, are in the main parallel, although there are striking differences in language. S. Matthew makes several insertions : vv. 11, 12; 27, 28 corresponding to Luke xvii. 24 and 37 ; and 37-41 corresponding to Luke xvii. 26-30, 34, 35.

S. Luke, on the other hand, makes some omissions, notably vv. 21 and 22 of S. Mark. In the discourse in ch. xvii. S. Luke has besides the parallels to S. Matthew's insertions, two verses, 25 and 33, which are parallel to Mark viii. 31 and 35. Since, however, these verses of S. Mark have closer parallels in Luke ix. 22, 24, there is every probability that the discourse in ch. xvii. is not derived from the Marcan tradition. After ver. 32 S. Mark has in xiii. 33 37 'a triple injunction to watchfulness, ἀγρυπνεῖτε (ver. 33), γρηγορεῖτε (ver. 35), and γρηγορεῖτε (ver. 37) in connexion with a single short parable or trope illustrating the duty.' In place of this S. Matthew has three parables, which more or less closely illustrate the injunctions in S. Mark. All three parables have parallels in S. Luke in other connexions, the two first in ch. xii. and the third in ch. xix. Probably therefore S. Luke in chs. xii. and xvii. and S. Matthew in ch. xxiv. have derived their common matter from the same non-Marcan source, and in ch. xxi. S. Luke has omitted certain parts of the Marcan tradition because of their similarity to the matter which he has already inserted.

If the foregoing examination of passages, which has been based almost entirely on Mr. Woods' essay, be even in its main features correct, it is clear that the conclusion to which it leads is one of the greatest importance. For it proves that the difference between the canonical Gospel and the 'Urmarcus' must be at any rate much smaller than has often been supposed.

The two must have been identical both in matter, with the possible exception of one or two passages, and in the order in which that matter was presented. There is no room left for changes more radical than the insertion or omission of a sentence here and there, an alteration in the turn of a phrase, the addition of a word or expression to expand, illustrate, or explain. In a word, the differences must have been almost entirely linguistic. Why then, we naturally ask, is it necessary to suppose that any change at all has taken place? May not the Gospel which we possess be word for word the same as that which was written down by the Evangelist? The reason why we cannot admit this is as

Occasional signs of posteriority in the language of S. Mark.
follows. Although a comparison of the language of S. Mark with that of the other Synoptists confirms on the whole our belief in the priority of the second Gospel, it does not confirm it in every particular. There are signs of posteriority as well as of priority. Again and again throughout the Gospel, but with special frequency in the last few chapters, S. Mark's language differs from that of S. Matthew and S. Luke in points in which the two last agree. This agreement of the two later Evangelists against the earlier constitutes one of the greatest difficulties of the Synoptic problem. As an average example of its nature and extent we may take the verses which describe how the disciples were plucking corn on the sabbath.

Matt. xii. 1, 2.	Mark ii. 23, 24.	Luke vi. 1, 2.
Ἐν ἐκείνῳ τῷ καιρῷ ἐπορεύθη ὁ Ἰησοῦς τοῖς σάββασιν διὰ τῶν σπορίμων· οἱ δὲ μαθηταὶ αὐτοῦ ἐπείνασαν, καὶ ἤρξαντο τίλλειν στάχυας ΚΑΙ ΕΣΘΙειν. οἱ ΔΕ Φαρισαῖοι ἰδόντες ΕΙΠΑΝ αὐτῷ· Ἰδοὺ οἱ μαθηταί σου ποιοῦσιν ὃ οὐκ ἔξεστιν ΠΟΙΕΙΝ ἐν σαββάτῳ.	Καὶ ἐγένετο αὐτὸν ἐν τοῖς σάββασιν διαπορεύεσθαι διὰ τῶν σπορίμων, καὶ οἱ μαθηταὶ αὐτοῦ ἤρξαντο ὁδὸν ποιεῖν τίλλοντες τοὺς στάχυας. καὶ οἱ Φαρισαῖοι ἔλεγον αὐτῷ· Ἴδε τί ποιοῦσιν τοῖς σάββασιν ὃ οὐκ ἔξεστιν;	Ἐγένετο δὲ ἐν σαββάτῳ διαπορεύεσθαι αὐτὸν διὰ σπορίμων, καὶ ἔτιλλον οἱ μαθηταὶ αὐτοῦ τοὺς στάχυας ΚΑΙ ΗΣΘΙον ψώχοντες ταῖς χερσίν. τινὲς ΔΕ τῶν Φαρισαίων ΕΙΠΑΝ, Τί ποιεῖτε ὃ οὐκ ἔξεστιν [ΠΟΙΕΙΝ] τοῖς σάββασιν;

In these two verses the language of the three Evangelists is to a large extent identical, and where it is not so, S. Mark is usually supported by either S. Matthew or S. Luke. Still there is a residuum of points in which these two are agreed against him. This agreement is of two kinds. On the one hand the Marcan narrative contains certain words which are absent from S. Matthew and S. Luke; on the other, the two later Evangelists have in common some words which do not appear in S. Mark. The former class of words is naturally of much less importance than the latter, since two writers who use with freedom a common document are far more likely to modify the language of that document by the same omissions from it, than by the same additions to it. In the passage just quoted the points which S. Matthew and S. Luke agree in omitting are very small and unimportant, practically consisting of nothing more than the phrase ὁδὸν ποιεῖν, which may so easily have been omitted by the later Evangelists as an unnecessary detail, that it is quite superfluous to seek any other explanation of its appearance in S. Mark alone. In other passages, however, as will be seen presently, some of the peculiarities of S. Mark cannot be so easily accounted for. Again, the identical insertions of S. Matthew and S. Luke are also small and unimportant: they consist of the words καὶ ἐσθίειν (ἤσθιον), δέ, εἶπαν, and ποιεῖν, the last word being omitted in some of the best manuscripts of S. Luke. But one passage can give no idea of the nature of the problem presented by these minute differences between S. Mark and his fellow Evangelists. It is the continual recurrence of such points that demands explanation: a few instances might be attributed to accident; but with each addition to the number of cases the adequacy of this explanation proportionately decreases.

Of the various theories which, besides the 'Urmarcus' hypothesis, have been put forward to account for these Theories to explain these 'secondary features.'

(1) Weiss.

'secondary features' of S. Mark, as they are called, the best known are probably those of Weiss and Simons.

Weiss holds that in compiling his Gospel S. Mark made use not only of the Petrine preaching, but also of the 'Logia[1],' a collection of discourses mingled with narrative, which is generally supposed to lie behind the canonical S. Matthew, and to have been used also by S. Luke. In some cases, he thinks, the first and third Gospels have preserved the language of the Logia more faithfully than S. Mark has, and in this way the coincidences between them are explained. The theory is an awkward one, since it postulates a double use of the Logia, which must have been employed by the compiler of the first Gospel once in its original form, and once as incorporated into S. Mark. But there are still more serious objections to the view. In the first place, it is extremely unlikely that S. Mark would use the Logia and then omit from it the discourses which were its most characteristic feature. Again, the extreme difficulty of determining what parts of S. Mark were taken from the Logia and what from the Petrine preaching gives rise to a great deal of arbitrariness in the decision of the question[2]. Further, whatever may have been the exact extent of the Logia, it is not probable that it contained the history of the Passion, so that, as Holtzmann says, the 'Apostolic source dries up just where it might be called upon to render most important service[3].'

(2) Simons.

The other theory, that of Professor Simons of Bonn,

---

[1] The term is derived from the saying of Papias that Ματθαῖος . . . . Ἑβραΐδι διαλέκτῳ τὰ Λόγια συνεγράψατο, ἡρμήνευσε δ' αὐτὰ ὡς ἦν δυνατὸς ἕκαστος. For a statement of the problems connected with this document, see the articles by Dr. Sanday referred to on p. 27.

[2] It is almost impossible to understand the principles on which Weiss reconstructs the Logia. It seems as if one of his main criteria were the word ἰδού. Wherever that occurs he refers the passage to the 'apostolic source,' and claims superiority for the Gospel (usually S. Matthew) which contains it. Cf. his *Marcusevangelium*, on (e. g.) iii. 32, ix. 4, x. 33.

[3] *O. c.*, p. 357.

has of late years found many supporters on the Continent, among them Professor Holtzmann, who has in consequence given up his allegiance to the 'Urmarcus' hypothesis. Simons accounts for the coincidences between the first and third Gospels by supposing that the writer of S. Luke was acquainted with the canonical S. Matthew. The great charm of this theory is its simplicity. But it is the fate of simple theories on the Synoptic question to break down when applied to the facts, and in this case there seems to be no exception to the rule. To begin with, it makes it necessary to assign a very late date to S. Luke—both Simons and Holtzmann relegate it to the second century—and also it gives no adequate explanation of the great divergences between S. Matthew and S. Luke, some of which, as for instance those in the Sermon on the Mount, are only just compatible with the hypothesis that the two versions are independent modifications of the same original narrative, while on Simons' theory the task of accounting for them is rendered harder still. It is indeed contended that S. Luke only used S. Matthew slightly and cursorily, quoting perhaps from memory. But we have already seen that his coincidences with S. Matthew mainly consist of small linguistic points; and these are just what such a view fails to explain.

The only remaining alternative seems to be the 'Urmarcus' theory. And in order to determine the nature and extent of the changes which have taken place in the Gospel, it will be necessary first to attempt the difficult task of classifying the 'secondary features,' or, as they should be called in order not to beg the question of their posteriority beforehand, the 'peculiarities' of S. Mark.

At the risk of appearing to draw arbitrary distinctions we must first examine some supposed secondary features, which in reality are not secondary at all.

(3) The 'Urmarcus' hypothesis.

Classification of Marcan peculiarities.
(1) Secondary features wrongly so called.

(*a*) Linguistic points. In place of an inelegant or obscure expression of S. Mark, S. Matthew and S. Luke often agree in having one which is free from these defects [1].

They simplify a needlessly complicated phrase [2], add for clearness a definite subject to a sentence [3], and substitute a better equivalent for an incorrect term, or an Aramaic word, or a Latinism which detracts from the purity of the Marcan style [4]. Again, they insert a word or phrase to bring out clearly an idea implied but not expressed in S. Mark's narrative [5]. Another point in which the first and third Gospels frequently combine against the second is in having εἶπεν in place of λέγει. There are nine cases where this occurs, besides four in which S. Matthew alone can be appealed to, there being no Lucan parallel to the passage [6]. The last is a change that was almost inevitable unless S. Matthew

---

[1] Mark ii. 16 οἱ γραμματεῖς ... ἔλεγον ... ὅτι μετὰ τῶν τελωνῶν καὶ ἁμαρτωλῶν ἐσθίει καὶ πίνει. S. Matthew (ix. 11) and S. Luke (v. 30) make the statement into a question and change ὅτι to διατί.
Mark iv. 11 ὑμῖν τὸ μυστήριον δέδοται τῆς βασιλείας τοῦ Θεοῦ. The other Evangelists (Matt. xiii. 11, Luke viii. 10) insert γνῶναι and change τὸ μυστήριον to τὰ μυστήρια, thus slightly altering the meaning of the saying, but making it easier to understand.
Mark xi. 32 ἀλλὰ εἴπωμεν· ἐξ ἀνθρώπων. Matt. xxi. 25, and Luke xx. 6. have ἐάν for ἀλλά.
Mark xii. 37 λέγει ... πόθεν. Matt. xxii. 45, Luke xx. 44 καλεῖ ... πῶς.

[2] Mark iv. 10 οἱ περὶ αὐτὸν σὺν τοῖς δώδεκα. Matt. xiii. 10, Luke viii. 9 οἱ μαθηταὶ αὐτοῦ.
Mark ix. 6 ἔκφοβοι ἐγένοντο. Matt. xvii. 6, Luke ix. 34 ἐφοβήθησαν.
Mark xiii. 5 ἤρξατο λέγειν. Matt. xxiv. 4, Luke xxi. 5 εἶπε.
Mark xv. 41 ὅτε ἦν ἐν τῇ Γαλιλαίᾳ. Matt. xxvii. 55, Luke xxiii. 49 ἀπὸ τῆς Γαλιλαίας.

[3] With Mark xii. 3 cf. Matt. xxi. 35, Luke xx. 10 οἱ γεωργοί.
With Mark xii. 12 cf. Matt. xxi. 45 οἱ ἀρχιερεῖς καὶ οἱ Φαρισαῖοι, Luke xx. 19 οἱ γραμματεῖς καὶ οἱ ἀρχιερεῖς.

[4] Mark vi. 14 βασιλεύς. Matt. xiv. 1, Luke ix. 7 τετράρχης.
Mark x. 51 ῥαββονί. Matt. xx. 30, Luke xviii. 41 Κύριε.
Mark xv. 39 κεντυρίων. Matt. xxvii. 54. Luke xxiii. 47 ἑκατόνταρχος.

[5] With Mark ii. 23 cf. Matt. xii. 1 καὶ ἐσθίειν, Luke vi. 1 καὶ ἤσθιον.
With Mark iv. 41 cf. Matt. viii. 27, Luke viii. 25 ἐθαύμασαν.
With Mark xiv. 65 cf. Matt. xxvi. 68, Luke xxii. 64 τίς ἐστιν ὁ παίσας σε ;

[6] Mark ii. 5 = Matt. xi. 2, Luke v. 20 ; Mark ii. 17 = Matt. ix. 12, Luke

and S. Luke had been particularly anxious to perpetuate one of the distinctive peculiarities of S. Mark's style, namely, the use of the present instead of the past tense. Again, there are cases where a vivid and forcible expression seems to have been softened down in the later Gospels with the view of giving a greater flow and smoothness to the narrative [1]. It is a significant fact that we never find S. Matthew and S. Luke agreeing against S. Mark in the support of a harder or less elegant reading. So the question arises, Which is the more probable, that these harder readings of S. Mark are later in origin than the easier ones of S. Matthew and S. Luke, or that S. Matthew and S. Luke have chanced to make the same alterations in the language of S. Mark in a certain number of cases, a number which is very small in proportion to the frequency with which they modify that language in different ways? It can hardly be denied that the balance of probability is in favour of the latter hypothesis.

We must also not forget another fact which textual criticism has of late years brought out with increasing force. Early copyists of the New Testament books must have used considerable freedom with the texts which lay before them [2]. A notorious example of this is found in the 'Western' readings, especially in the case of S. Luke and of the Acts. And if manuscripts which we possess

---

v. 31; Mark iii. 4 = Matt. xii. 11, Luke vi. 9; Mark iii. 34 = Matt. xii. 48, Luke viii. 21; Mark ix. 5 = Matt. xvii. 4, Luke ix. 33; Mark ix. 19 Matt. xvii. 17, Luke ix. 41; Mark x. 23 = Matt. xix. 23, Luke xviii. 24; Mark x. 27 = Matt. xix. 26, Luke xviii. 27; Mark x. 42 = Matt. xx. 25, Luke xxii. 25.

The four cases in which εἶπεν is found in S. Matthew only are Mark vii. 28 = Matt. xv. 27; Mark viii. 1 = Matt. xv. 32; Mark viii. 17 Matt. xvi. 8; Mark xi. 22 = Matt. xxi. 21.

[1] Mark i. 10 σχιζομένους = Matt. iii. 16 ἀνεῴχθησαν, Luke iii. 21 ἀνεῳχθῆναι; Mark ix. 18 ἴσχυσαν = Matt. xvii. 16, Luke ix. 40 ἠδυνήθησαν; Mark xiii. 2 οὐ μὴ καταλυθῇ = Matt. xxiv. 2, Luke xxi. 6 οὐ καταλυθήσεται. It is worth noting also how the hyperbolical expression in Mark x. 30 ἑκατονταπλασίονα, is softened down to πολλαπλασίονα in Matt. xix. 29, Luke xviii. 30.

[2] Cf. Sanday, Bampton Lectures, pp. 295 f.

E

give evidence of such a tendency on the part of copyists, it is, to say the least, possible that many changes were made in the first few copies of the Gospels which have left no traces of themselves in extant codices. Thus the well-known tendency to alter the words of one Gospel into harmony with another may well account for some of the coincidences between S. Matthew and S. Luke. Still, to lay much stress on this consideration is dangerous, since, like so many similar arguments, it is a double-edged weapon. For if in some instances a fictitious agreement in language between S. Matthew and S. Luke has been produced by a copyist, the possibility must also be recognized that peculiarities of S. Mark have been in the same way obliterated in order to bring the second Gospel into verbal agreement with the two others.

(*b*) Supposed omissions of our Lord's sayings.

(*b*) There is a second class of Marcan peculiarities far more important and interesting than those which have just been dealt with. Occasionally it seems as if whole sentences had fallen out of the text of S. Mark. A frequently quoted example is the saying of our Lord to the Syro-Phoenician woman, 'I was not sent but unto the lost sheep of the house of Israel,' which is preserved by S. Matthew but not by S. Mark[1]: S. Luke does not record the incident. The words are so striking, so undoubtedly genuine, that it a great temptation to suppose that they were included in the original text of the second Gospel. But then it is difficult to explain why they should have fallen out. Moreover, it is to be noticed that S. Matthew's account of the interview with the woman, although in the main parallel to S. Mark's, has yet in point of language little in common with it, so that unless we suppose that the variations of the first Evangelist are merely arbitrary, we can hardly help concluding that he was influenced by some other version

---

[1] Matt. xv. 24, cf. Mark vii. 24–30.

of the story, either written or oral. May not the differences be explained by the supposition that S. Matthew
incorporates into his own narrative elements both from
the Marcan version, and from an oral account current
in Jerusalem, which would be more likely than the
Petrine teaching to preserve a saying directly referring
to our Saviour's mission to the Jewish people ? The
objections which exist against the 'oral' theory as
a whole do not apply to its occasional appearance as
a factor in the explanation of the Synoptic difficulties.
And if, as is rendered probable by the known habits of
the Jews of that age, there was current in Palestine
a definite cycle of oral teaching, it would have been
strange if it did not sometimes coincide with the teaching
of S. Peter at Rome.

There are other sayings recorded in S. Matthew, which
are probably to be attributed to the same source, especially
as they are absent both from S. Mark and from S. Luke.
Such are, ' Go ye and learn what this meaneth, I desire
mercy and not sacrifice [1];' ' Verily I say unto you, Except
ye turn and become as little children. ye shall in no wise
enter into the kingdom of heaven [2];' ' Verily I say unto
you, that ye which have followed Me, in the regeneration
when the Son of man shall sit on the throne of His
glory, ye shall also sit upon twelve thrones, judging the
twelve tribes of Israel [3].'

It would greatly simplify the task of Synoptic criticism
could all the peculiarities of S. Mark be explained in
a similar manner. Unfortunately, however, there remain
certain peculiarities which do not readily lend themselves
to any such explanations, and these constitute the 'secondary
features ' proper, which it seems only possible to account
for by the supposition that they represent changes made
in the text at some date after it was used by the writers
of the other Gospels. Two classes of secondary features

[2] Second-
ary fea-
tures
proper.

[1] ix. 13.   [2] xviii. 3.   [3] xix. 28.

can be more or less clearly distinguished, while there are others of a less definite character.

Context supplements [1]. A common feature of the style of the second Gospel is the presence of short explanatory sentences, connecting links in the narrative, which seem inserted merely to make it more intelligible. As a rule these sentences convey no new information, and are couched almost wholly in the words of the immediate context. The account of the healing of the paralytic in the second chapter contains some excellent examples, five of them occurring in four consecutive verses, and all absent from the parallel narratives of the other Synoptists. In ver. 15 we read the words, 'for they were many and they followed Him'; in ver. 16, 'when they saw that He was eating with the sinners and publicans'; in ver. 18, 'And John's disciples and the Pharisees were fasting,' and 'as long as they have the bridegroom with them they cannot fast.' If these had been in the original text of S. Mark, why should both the other Evangelists have agreed to omit them all? There is nothing, as far as we can see, in the words or construction which could give offence.

Other instances of such supplements are not infrequent, although perhaps none are so clear and definite as those just mentioned [2]. Great caution is needed in the selection of examples, since it is impossible to assign all such explanatory sentences to the hand of an editor of the Gospel. They are to a large extent inherent in the style of the Gospel, as may be seen by reference to passages where the other Evangelists perpetuate them in their own narratives. The general circumstantiality of S. Mark's style naturally leads to the repetition of words and clauses [3].

---

[1] This term, as well as much of what is said on the subject, is due to a lecture by Prof. Armitage Robinson on 'The Editor's Hand in S. Mark.'

[2] Cf. e.g. vi. 35 ; vii. 19 ; viii. 1 ; ix. 34 ; x. 27 ; xii. 15, 21, 23 ; xiv. 16.

[3] Cf. e.g. i. 25, 26 ; ii. 7, 8 ; iv. 5, 30–32 ; v. 28 ; viii. 12 ; ix. 17 ; x. 8 ; xi. 28, 29 ; xiv. 21.

Supplements added to heighten the sense of the narrative or to enhance contrasts. It is very striking how frequently words like πᾶς, ἅπας, πολύς, μέγας and ὀλίγος, and again conjunctions and adverbs such as ἀλλά, ὧδε and πάλιν occur in S. Mark, while they are absent in the other Synoptists: πᾶς (or ἅπας) occurs sixty-nine times in S. Mark and in nineteen cases it is unattested by S. Matthew and S. Luke, account being only taken of those passages in which one or other of the later Evangelists closely follows in other respects the language of the earlier [1]. Similarly of fifty-nine instances of πολύς twenty-one are unattested [2].

So the conclusion is suggested that these two classes of supplements are additions to the original text of S. Mark, and the work of an editor whose aim was to make the Gospel at once more intelligible and more interesting to its readers by the insertion of explanatory clauses, connecting links between the sentences, and words intended to bring into still stronger relief the light and shade of the already vivid narrative. In carrying out this design he seems to have followed closely the style and vocabulary of S. Mark, and only to have intensified its peculiarities, thus giving to the revised Gospel such an appearance of unity that were S. Matthew and S. Luke not extant no one would ever have suspected that it was not wholly the work of the same hand.

But was this the sole object of the editor or only a part of his object? That is to say, did he go further and add any really independent matter of his own? The more important passages peculiar to S. Mark have already been examined in some detail, and it has been seen that there is no evidence to prove that they were not in the original text. Probably, however, there will always be some doubt

---

[1] i. 5, 32; ii. 12; iv. 11, 32; v. 40; vi. 30, 33, 50; vii. 14, 23; x. 44; xi. 17; xii. 28; xiii. 4, 23; xiv. 36, 53, 64.

[2] i. 34; ii. 15; iii. 8, 10; iv. 33; v. 10, 21, 23, 24, 26, 38, 43; vi. 2, 33, 35; ix. 12; x. 48; xii. 5, 41 twice; xv. 3.

as to the originality of one or two verses, especially the account of the ceremonial washings of the Pharisees (vii. 2–4), which on the one hand reads like an explanatory gloss such as an editor might insert, and on the other may equally well have been omitted by S. Matthew as unnecessary for his Jewish readers. Leaving therefore out of sight such passages as this, let us see whether there are any indications of fresh matter being added in smaller points. It is of course most improbable that of the vivid details so characteristic of S. Mark all those which are not found in the other Evangelists are to be attributed to a later editor of the Gospel. On the other hand the possibility must be admitted that some are to be referred to him. There is, for instance, a passage where S. Matthew and S. Luke combine in a peculiar way against S. Mark. In the account of the feeding of the five thousand S. Mark has the words 'two hundred pennyworth of bread,' while S. Matthew and S. Luke have merely 'food' ($\beta\rho\acute{\omega}\mu\alpha\tau\alpha$). Why should the later Evangelists agree to substitute a vague word for the more precise expression of S. Mark? It is far more probable that the word in the original text of the Gospel was $\beta\rho\acute{\omega}\mu\alpha\tau\alpha$ and that this was altered by an editor who had before him an independent account of the event. When we turn to the narrative of S. John, the words 'two hundred pennyworth of bread is not sufficient for them' make us suspect what the source of this independent information was [1]. Our suspicions are confirmed by a study of another of the few passages where the narratives of the Synoptists and of S. John coincide. In the story of the anointing at Bethany, S. Mark and S. John both use the expression 'pistic nard,' the exact

(c Possible insertions of independent matter from a Johannean source.

[1] Mark vi. 37; Matt. xiv. 15; Luke ix. 13; John vi. 7. The use by S. Mark and S John of the word $\dot{\alpha}\nu\alpha\pi\acute{\iota}\pi\tau\epsilon\iota\nu$ for 'to sit down,' in contrast with the $\dot{\alpha}\nu\alpha\kappa\lambda\acute{\iota}\nu\epsilon\sigma\theta\alpha\iota$ of S. Matthew and $\kappa\alpha\tau\alpha\kappa\lambda\acute{\iota}\nu\epsilon\iota\nu$ of S. Luke, is perhaps too small a point to be insisted on. For another linguistic coincidence between the two, cf. the use of $\pi\alpha\acute{\iota}\epsilon\iota\nu$ in Mark xiv. 47. John xviii. 10. Matt. xxvi. 51 and Luke xxii. 50 have $\pi\alpha\tau\acute{\alpha}\sigma\sigma\epsilon\iota\nu$.

meaning of which has always been a matter of controversy. Both mention the value of the ointment, S. John saying that it was worth 'three hundred pence,' S. Mark 'more than three hundred pence,' while S. Matthew only informs us vaguely that it 'might have been sold for much.' Both preserve in almost the same words our Lord's command to 'leave the woman alone' (S. Mark ἄφετε αὐτήν, S. John ἄφες αὐτήν)[1]. To assert that these coincidences imply that the editor of S. Mark knew the Gospel of S. John would be to go further than the evidence warrants, but they do suggest what is in itself by no means improbable, namely, that he was influenced by the Johannean cycle of teaching, which is generally believed to have preceded the actual composition of the fourth Gospel.

It seems also possible to discern traces of an editor in quite a different connexion, namely, in the discourse about the end of the world, which is recorded in chapter xiii. The difficult question of the origin and mutual relationship of the various discourses on this subject, contained in the three Synoptists, has been already mentioned. All that concerns us here is the difference in the language of the three Evangelists in certain parallel passages. According to S. Matthew it is foretold that the Second Advent will be 'immediately after the tribulation of those days,' S. Mark dates it more vaguely 'in those days, after that tribulation'; while S. Luke gives no note of time whatever[2]. Again, with regard to the fall of Jerusalem, S. Matthew has the words, 'When therefore ye see the abomination of desolation, which was spoken of by Daniel the prophet, standing in the holy place'; S. Mark, 'But when ye see the abomination of desolation standing where he ought not'; S. Luke, 'But when ye see Jerusalem encompassed with armies[3].'

(d) Modifications of language in eschatological discourse.

---

[1] Mark xiv. 3-6; John xii. 3-7; Matt. xxvi. 6-10.
[2] Matt. xxiv. 29; Mark xiii. 24; Luke xxi. 25.
[3] Matt. xxiv. 15; Mark xiii. 14; Luke xxi. 20.

Such elaborate theories as to the dates of the Gospels have been built on these discourses, a strain has been laid on them so much greater than they will bear, that one feels a natural hesitation in appealing to them at all. But if 'abusus non tollit usum,' a comparison of the language of the three Evangelists suggests at first sight the conclusion that S. Matthew has preserved most closely the original report, which was modified to a certain extent by S. Mark and still more by S. Luke in order to bring it into harmony with later events. There appears a tendency in the two latter Gospels both to dissolve the immediate connexion between the fall of Jerusalem and the second Advent, and to make the references to the former more explicit[1]. This therefore is one of the puzzling cases which seem to conflict with the general priority of S. Mark to S. Matthew. And yet, on the assumption that one or two slight alterations have been made in the text of S. Mark, that Gospel still preserves its originality. In fact, the changes in question may really have consisted of nothing more than the omission of the word εὐθέως in ver. 24, since as to the relative priority of the words ὅπου οὐ δεῖ and ἐν τόπῳ ἁγίῳ critics are not agreed; Meyer, for instance, defending the Marcan phrase, and Weiss the Matthaean[2].

To sum up, therefore, it seems as if the work of an editor of S. Mark may be discerned in four different connexions: (*a*) in explanatory supplements; (*b*) in single words added to heighten effects and strengthen contrasts; (*c*) in a few details added from an independent source, which is probably Johannean; (*d*) in the change of a word or two in the

---

[1] Cf. Mark xiii. 19 with Luke xxi. 23, 24.

[2] Further signs of posteriority in S. Mark have been thought to exist in the words πρῶτον in xiii. 10 and πᾶσιν τοῖς ἔθνεσιν in xi. 17. But the former seems to make no real difference to the meaning of the verse (cf. Matt. xxiv. 14), and the latter (from Is. lvi. 7) has a special appropriateness when it is remembered that the words were probably spoken in the court of the Gentiles. See Weiss *ad locum*.

eschatological discourse designed to bring it into closer harmony with current events.

Do these constitute the sum total of the editorial changes? Probably not, and yet when the attempt is made to determine which of the other peculiarities of S. Mark represent later modifications of and additions to the text of the original Gospel, and which are due simply to a free handling of it by S. Matthew and S. Luke, the arguments for each view are so evenly balanced that it seems better to leave the question an open one for the present. Closer study of the text or the discovery of new manuscripts may, and probably will, throw fresh light on the methods of the editor and the extent of the changes he introduced, but he would be a bold man who in the present condition of our knowledge would undertake to reconstruct the text of the 'Urmarcus.' And if the result here arrived at seems meagre and disappointing, if we are inclined to reject any theory of the history of S. Mark's Gospel which is not, like Horace's wise man, 'in se ipso totus, teres atque rotundus,' it will be well for us to remind ourselves that at least in the sphere of New Testament criticism the usual way of attaining exactness and completeness is to ignore the presence of inconvenient facts which will not adapt themselves to preconceived theories.

Two more questions with regard to the editor of S. Mark still remain, but they can only be treated briefly here. The first is, 'What was his probable date?' the second, 'Can he be identified with the author of the last twelve verses?'

The answer to the first question depends partly on the date assigned to the original Gospel, partly on the amount of importance attached to the supposed alterations in the text of the eschatological discourse. If we may follow the tradition preserved in Irenaeus, S. Mark composed his Gospel soon after the death of S. Peter, an event which, according to the usual reckoning, took place in the year

Probable date of the editor.

67 [1]. Other authorities, such as Clement of Alexandria, Origen, and Eusebius, tell us that S. Mark wrote during the lifetime of the Apostle. In any case the Gospel was probably written within a few years of the death of S. Peter, either before or after. The 'terminus a quo' we have no means of fixing; the 'terminus ad quem' would naturally be the year 70, the date of the fall of Jerusalem [2]. Allowing a sufficient interval after its publication for copies of it to come into the hands of the compilers of the first and third Gospels, we may hazard c. 73–76 as the most probable date of the redaction. For if we may draw any inference from the omission by the editor of the εὐθέως which S. Matthew preserves, it suggests that he was engaged in revising the Gospel after Jerusalem had fallen, but not so long after as to make the vaguer expression, 'in those days,' irreconcilable with the facts. At any rate it seems certain that the second Gospel (as indeed was the case with the first and third also) reached its final form within the lifetime of the generation to which our Lord had addressed His discourse. Otherwise, since the compilers of all three Gospels appear not to hesitate to make slight alterations and omissions in our Lord's discourses, in order to bring them into closer correspondence with the events which they seemed to predict, all of them would hardly have preserved the saying, 'This generation shall not pass away till all be fulfilled,' since that seems to refer not only to the fall of Jerusalem, but also to the Second Coming.

[1] Cf. Ramsay, *The Church in the Roman Empire*, c. xiii. Prof. Ramsay accepts the genuineness of 1 Peter, but maintains that it cannot have been written before about A.D. 80. If this be so, 'the usual view according to which Peter perished at Rome in the Neronian persecution, is not correct.' In this case we must reject Irenaeus' tradition, and hold that the Gospel was composed some years before the death of the Apostle.

[2] The parenthetical warning of the Evangelist in xiii. 14, ὁ ἀναγινώσκων νοείτω, might lead us to conclude that he was writing during the period of expectation between the fall of Giscala at the end of 67 and the appearance of Titus before the walls of Jerusalem at the beginning of 70.

With regard to the second question menti ned above it has already been shown that the last twelve verses of the Gospel did not form part of the original text. It is extremely improbable that S. Mark intended ver. 8 to be the conclusion of his Gospel. No writer of Greek would have ended a paragraph with the words ἐφοβοῦντο γάρ; no historian would have concluded his work with a minute detail of an unimportant incident; no Evangelist would have closed the joyful account of the Resurrection with words which strike a note of unmitigated fear. We may assume, therefore, either that S. Mark left his Gospel unfinished, or, with more probability, that the end of the papyrus roll on which the Gospel was originally written perished at an extremely early date. Under these circumstances it would be a natural supposition that the editor who revised the text of the Gospel, being possessed of independent sources of information, added also a conclusion of his own. In favour of such a hypothesis are the contents of the verses in question, which while in general harmony with the accounts in the other Gospels do not seem to be based on them [1]. On the other hand, there are two objections against it. In the first place, while some of the oldest manuscripts omit the concluding verses entirely, there are no traces of any corresponding hesitation to accept the editor's additions to the text of the Gospel itself, and secondly, none of the peculiarities of style which characterize those additions are to be found in the passage where we should expect to see them most strongly exhibited.

The editor not to be identified with the author of the last twelve verses.

---

[1] Ver. 9 seems to refer to the appearance to Mary Magdalene recorded in John xx. 14 17; ver. 10 is in agreement with John xx. 18, but the fourth Evangelist does not mention the incredulity of the disciples recorded in ver. 11, which, however, seems to be alluded to in Luke xxiv. 11; vv. 12 13 probably give a condensed account of the walk to Emmaus, but a late writer who drew solely on the canonical Gospels for his information would have been careful not to contradict Luke xxiv. 34 by adding 'neither believed they them' in ver. 13; ver. 15 must refer to the appearance recorded in Luke xxiv. 36-42, although ὕστερον would naturally suggest a later event. With ver. 18, cf. Acts xxviii. 3-7, an incident which may well have been fresh in the memory of the writer.

The explanatory clauses, the heightened contrasts are both absent, and the verses convey the impression that they are from the hand of one who had considerable mastery over the Greek language, while the editor's own supplements and, still more, the apparent absence of any attempt on his part to enrich the vocabulary or improve the style of the Gospel itself, as, for instance, by the removal of anacolutha, forbid us to entertain the idea he was in any degree a stylist.

On the whole then it is best to regard the last verses of S. Mark not as the work of the editor, but as a still later addition, which perhaps originally formed the conclusion of an independent Gospel. Mr. F. C. Conybeare's discovery of an Armenian manuscript of the tenth century[1], in which the name of 'Ariston the elder' is prefixed to the verses, would enable us to assign them to the last years of the first century, could we be sure, in the first place, that any real importance can be attached to the evidence of a single codex, and that such a late one, and, secondly, that the Ariston in question can be identified with a certain Aristion, 'a disciple of the Lord,' who is mentioned by Papias as one of his informants, and who also, so Eusebius implies, was the author of certain 'narratives of the words of the Lord' (διηγήσεις τῶν τοῦ Κυρίου λόγων)[2]. But in default of further testimony this solution of the problem must remain a brilliant and attractive conjecture. There is no *a priori* reason against it: what we require is stronger evidence for it.

[1] See *Expositor*, Oct., 1893.   [2] Euseb. *H. E.* iii. 39.

PART III.

Purpose and Characteristics of the Gospel.

MANY of the peculiar features of the Gospel of S. Mark
have been already noticed in the course of the preceding
discussion, but as some of them seem to require a more
definite treatment, it may be convenient to gather up here
the threads of what has been said, and to consider (*a*) the
object of the Gospel and the leading ideas which run
through it, (*b*) the plan, (*c*) the style, (*d*) the place of the
Gospel in the economy of revelation.

(*a*) The Object. S. Mark, as we have seen, wrote for
Gentile Christians, and especially for the Romans. With
the growth of the Church the need began to be felt of
an authoritative written account of our Lord's life, and
the faithful follower and disciple of S. Peter had peculiar
capacities and opportunities for compiling such a record.
'Mark,' says Weiss, 'first undertook to convert into coin
(*verwerthen*) all the treasured-up reminiscences which were
placed at his disposal by communications from a prominent
eye-witness belonging to the innermost circle of the companions of Jesus, and with the help of those oldest
records to sketch out a general picture of the life of Christ,
which might proclaim to the Church the joyful news of
the appearance of the Messiah in Him [1].' Indications
of the Gentilic character of the Gospel may be found in
the general absence of quotations from and references to the
Old Testament [2], as well as in the translation or paraphrase
of Aramaic words [3], and the explanation of Jewish customs [4]

The object and leading ideas of the Gospel.

---

[1] *Marcusevangelium,* p. 21.
[2] After the introductory quotations from Malachi and Isaiah the O. T.
is never quoted in the Gospel except by our Lord Himself.
[3] iii. 17, 22 ; v. 41 ; vii. 11 ; ix. 43 ; xiv. 36 ; xv. 22, 34.
[4] vii. 1–4 ; xiv. 12 ; xv. 6, 42.

and Jewish opinions, such as the peculiar tenets of the Sadducees [1]. It may not even be fanciful to see in a few references to things specifically Roman, traces of its Roman origin [2].

In the days when the *Tendenzkritik* was rife, various endeavours were made to assign a narrow and partisan aim to the Gospel, but the contradictoriness of the results arrived at showed the futility of such attempts. Hilgenfeld, for instance, found in S. Mark a mitigated Judaeo-Christianity, Volkmar, on the other hand, pure Paulinism; but the usual character assigned was that of 'neutrality,' a verdict which was equivalent to a confession of failure on the part of those critics who pronounced it.

The opening words of the Gospel, 'The Gospel of Jesus Christ the Son of God,' strike the keynote of the work [3]. The aim of S. Mark was to give to the world a living picture of Jesus, as Man, as the Messiah, as the Son of God; to record with direct simplicity the story of His life, death, and resurrection, leaving what may be called the theological interpretion of those facts to be brought out by the later Evangelists, and especially by S. John. The aspect of our Lord's Person and work which comes out most strongly in the Gospel is of one who was a living 'power of God unto salvation.' The force that went forth from Him was enough to heal those who touched but the border of His garment, and this apparently without any special act of will on His part [4]. He claims and exercises

---

[1] xii. 18.

[2] x. 12 seems to refer to the Roman custom of divorce; xii. 42 the 'quadrans'; xiii. 35 (cf. vi. 48, and contrast with Luke xii. 38), adoption of the Roman division of the night into four watches. In xv. 1 a knowledge of Pilate's official position seems to be assumed.

[3] It is true that there is a doubt as to the genuineness of the words 'the Son of God.' Westcott and Hort omit them in the text, but say that neither reading can be safely rejected. Since, however, the divine Sonship finds full recognition in the Gospel (cf. e.g. i. 11, 24, xiv. 61) the omission of the words makes no essential difference to the argument.

[4] v. 25-34; vi. 56.

supremacy alike over the physical and over the spiritual world. The stilling of the waters of the lake is immediately followed by the expulsion of the Legion from the Gadarene demoniac [1]. S. Mark seems indeed to lay especial stress on the power of Jesus over evil spirits [2]. The first miracle recorded in the Gospel is the healing of the man with the unclean spirit at Capernaum [3]; and particular mention is made of the quickness of the spirits to recognize our Lord [4].

To S. Mark our Lord is not primarily the Messiah as in S. Matthew, nor the Saviour as in S. Luke. Not that the Evangelist was indifferent to the fulfilment of the Old Testament in Christ. Besides the introductory quotations, he preserves many of our Lord's own allusions to the Scriptures and to the history of the Jews, emphasizes His recognition of the law [5], His assertion of its authority against that of the Pharisaic traditions which prevented obedience to it [6], and His jealousy for the sanctity of the Temple, even at the time when He was announcing its destruction [7]. Still, on the whole it is true, as Bishop Westcott says, that 'the living portraiture of Christ is offered in the clearness of His present energy, not as the fulfilment of the Past, nor even as the foundation of the Future. His acts prove that He is both, but this is a deduction from the narrative and not the subject of it [8].'

In accordance with this leading idea is the great prominence of incident over discourse, of miracle over parable in the second Gospel. S. Mark relates almost as many miracles as the other Synoptists, but only four

[1] iv. 35 ; v. 20.
[2] i. 23-28, 34, 39; iii. 11, 15, 22; v. 1 20; vi. 7, 13; vii. 25 30; ix. 17 27.
[3] i 23 28.
[4] i. 23, 34 ; iii. 11.
[5] e g. ii. 25, 26 ; ix. 12, 13 ; xii. 10, 11 ; xiv. 21, 27, 49.
[6] vii. 9, 13.
[7] xi. 15, 16 ; xiii. 2.
[8] *O. c.* ch. vii. p. 365.

parables [1]. The contrast in the first chapter between the detailed account of the healing of the demoniac at Capernaum, and the cursory notice of the teaching in the synagogue which precedes it, is eminently characteristic of the Evangelist's subordination of our Lord's words to His acts [2]. He seems indeed to aim at recording only such sayings and discourses as he could connect with a definite situation and illustrate through that situation, a fact which suggests that he was more concerned with our Lord's method of teaching than with the matter which He taught. The Gospel is as far as possible from being either a collection of discourses or a complete biographical record: it is a series of scenes.

The plan.   (*b*) The Plan. We have seen that S. Mark's chief concern was with the active ministry of the Lord, and this fact explains the omission of the story of His birth and infancy, a point which affords a strong contrast to the detailed narratives in S. Matthew and S. Luke. After only thirteen verses of introductory matter relating briefly the ministry of the Baptist [3], the Baptism, and the Temptation, the Evangelist plunges *in medias res* with the account of our Lord's arrival in Galilee. In its main outlines the Gospel is chronological; that is to say, it recounts the principal events of our Lord's life in the order in which they took place; but within those limits, and especially with regard to the different divisions of the ministry, there is considerable vagueness. S. Mark's interest was not in chronology: the notes of time which he gives are vague—'again,' 'after some days,' 'in those days.' Only on occasions is he more precise, as when

---

[1] 1. The sower (iv. 1-20); 2. The seed growing secretly (iv. 26-29), peculiar to S. Mark; 3. The mustard-seed (iv. 30-32); 4. The husbandmen (xii. 1-12).

[2] i. 21, 22, 23-28.

[3] The correspondence is worth noting between the contents of the second Gospel and the limits of the apostolic testimony which are laid down by S. Peter in Acts i. 22.

he dates the Transfiguration six days after S. Peter's confession, and again in his account of the events immediately preceding the Passion [1].

But if it is difficult to regard S. Mark's narrative as based on purely chronological principles, it is no less difficult to discover any one leading idea which can have guided the Evangelist in the selection and arrangement of his facts. Various schemes have been proposed, but all strike us as more or less arbitrary and unsatisfactory. It seems best, therefore, to abandon the endeavour to trace out a dogmatic plan in the Gospel, and to content ourselves with indicating one point which, whether the Evangelist as he wrote was conscious of it or not, is strongly brought before us by a study of the Marcan narrative. This point is the gradualness of our Lord's revelation of Himself as the Messiah. The earlier period of the ministry, when our Lord's popularity was scarcely clouded by the shadow of approaching opposition, is marked by great reserve on His part. He withdraws Himself from the multitude [2], and enjoins strict silence on the demoniacs whom He had healed, and who according to S. Mark were the first persons to recognize and openly proclaim Him as the Messiah [3]. The same desire for secrecy appears when He checks the exuberant gratitude of Jairus and his family, and treats with equal sternness the friends of the deaf mute at Decapolis, and the blind man at Bethsaida [4]. As, however, His fame spread and speculations as to His character and claims became rife, while the antagonism of the Pharisees increased in a corresponding ratio, He became less and less careful to preserve this attitude of concealment. The first exception to His rule of reserve seems to be found in the case of the Gadarene demoniac [5]. Up to

[1] ix. 2; xiv. 1, 12.   [2] i. 45; iii. 7.   [3] i. 24; iii. 11; v. 7.
[4] v. 43; vii. 36; viii. 26.   [5] v. 19, 20.

F

the time of His wanderings in the villages of Caesarea
Philippi, He had only hinted as it were at His Messiahship by His use of the title 'Son of Man[1];' the disciples
had received the commission not to announce Him as
the Messiah, but to preach repentance to the people,
and to heal the sick[2]. Not until after the great breach
with the Pharisees and the retirement into heathen lands[3]
—a retirement which probably gave opportunities for
closer and more continuous intercourse between the disciples and their Master—did the time arrive for S. Peter's
confession at Caesarea. Even then the disciples are com-
manded not to proclaim His Messiahship to the world,
and at the same time they are warned of His impending
Passion and Death[4]. - But the secret could no longer be
confined to the narrow circle of our Lord's immediate
followers. During the last journey to Jerusalem He was
openly hailed by Bartimaeus as the 'Son of David,' and
this time a rebuke was administered by the multitude
and not by our Lord Himself[5]. Then followed the
triumphal entry into the city, and the final proclamation
of the Messiahship first in a parable, afterwards openly[6].
'Again the high priest asked Him and saith unto Him,
Art thou the Christ, the Son of the Blessed? and Jesus
said, I am.'

Style.   (c) Style. The style of S. Mark is in perfect harmony
with the distinctive peculiarities of the 'Gospel of action.'
He has not the literary purity and finish of S. Luke,
and writes the ordinary Hellenistic Greek of his day,

[1] ii. 10, 28.   [2] vi. 12, 13.   [3] vii. 24 ; viii. 27.
[4] viii. 30, 31 ; cf. ix. 9.   [5] x. 48.
[6] xii. 1-9 ; xiv. 61. Holtzmann (*Einleitung*, p. 359) points out that in
S. Matthew our Lord is recognized as the Messiah from the beginning.
He is recognized by the Baptist and proclaimed by the voice from heaven
(iii. 14, 17; contrast Mark i. 11). Twice also S. Matthew omits the injunction of secrecy (cf. Matt. ix. 26, xv. 31 with Mark v. 43, vii. 36), and
he further obliterates the gradual character of the revelation by inserting
before S. Peter's confession the designation of our Lord by the blind and
afflicted as the ' Son of David,' and by the disciples as the ' Son of God.'

but with no special leaning towards Hebraistic constructions. In fact, actual Hebraisms are rare in the
Gospel[1], although the Evangelist does not shrink from
incorporating Aramaic words and expressions, to which,
however, he usually appends a Greek translation[2]. On
the other hand there is a striking number of Latin forms,
which seem to point to the Roman origin of the Gospel[3].
We have already seen how he uses colloquial and inelegant
words which were condemned by grammarians. Other
characteristics of Hellenistic Greek which appear in
S. Mark are the ' constructio ad sensum' in the use of
gender and number[4], the use of εἶναι with the participle
instead of the simple verb[5], the construction with ἵνα
in place of the infinitive[6], and a general neglect of the
fine distinctions which classical Greek drew with regard
to the meaning of a preposition when used with different
cases[7].

As regards the form and structure of the sentences,
they are as a rule simply co-ordinated with καί, for
which sometimes δέ is substituted without any apparent

---

[1] δύο δύο vi. 7 (cf. vi. 39, 40); βλέπειν ἀπό viii. 15, xii. 38. The nominative
with the article in place of the vocative, v. 41, ix. 25, xiv. 36; εἰ express-
ing a strong negative assertion, viii. 12. Possibly also there should be
included in the list redundant expressions such as οὗ . . . αὐτοῦ (i. 7, cf.
vii. 25), οἷος . . . τοιοῦτος (xiii. 19), οἷος . . . οὕτως (ix. 3).

[2] iii. 17; v. 41; vii. 11, 34; x. 46; xiv. 36; xv. 22, 34.

[3] σπεκουλάτωρ vi. 27; κεντυρίων xv. 39, 44, 45; ξέστης (sextarius) vii. 4.
These are peculiar to S. Mark. In common with other N. T. writers he
has κοδράντης (Matt.), κῆνσος (Matt.), φραγελλοῦν (Matt.), λεγεών (Matt.,
Luke), πραιτώριον (Matt., John, Acts), δηνάριον (Matt., Luke, John). To
these may perhaps be added κράββατος (John, Acts), and the expressions
τὸ ἱκανὸν ποιεῖν (xv. 15 = satisfacere, cf. Acts xvii. 9 ἱκανὸν λαμβάνειν),
ῥαπίσμασί τινα λαμβάνειν (xiv. 65 = verberibus aliquem accipere), and ὁδὸν
ποιεῖν (ii. 23 = iter facere).

[4] e.g. ii. 13; iii. 8; iv. 1; v. 24; ix. 15, 20; xiii. 14.

[5] e.g. i. 6, 22, and *passim.*

[6] e.g. iii. 9; v. 10, 18; vi. 25; vii. 26; ix. 9, 12, 18, 30; x. 35, 37. 51;
xi. 16; xiv. 35.

[7] e.g. ἐπί with the accusative when no thought of motion is involved;
ii. 14; iv. 38; xi. 2; xiii. 2; παρά iv. 1; v. 21; x. 46. Cf. the 'pregnant'
use of εἰς in i. 9; x. 10; xiii. 16.

intention on the part of the author to point a contrast[1]. Like S. John, S. Mark often resolves a single clause into two or more co-ordinate ones, instead of appending participles according to the ordinary Greek idiom[2]. In long sentences anacolutha are by no means a rarity[3]. Not infrequently we find in place of a pronoun the subject or principal word of the sentence repeated[4], but this is not so noticeable a feature of the second as it is of the fourth Gospel, and S. Mark can by no means be said to avoid pronouns, for the continual repetition of αὐτός is a distinctive characteristic of his style[5]. Sometimes again we find that the subject or the object of the sentence is completely absent[6]. They seem to have been so vividly present to the writer that he as it were passes them over unconsciously.

We may, perhaps, take these last two peculiarities, the repetition and omission of the subject, as representative of the two main features of S. Mark's style, circumstantiality and vividness. There is a breadth and completeness about his sentences which arises partly from the fact that he does not hesitate to repeat a word again and again in cases where a more finished Greek writer would have altered the phrase[7], partly from his fondness for explanatory clauses (some of which, however, as we have seen, are to be referred to a later hand), and most of all from his habit of coupling together similar phrases in order to heighten and define his meaning.

---

[1] e.g. in x. 1–7, 20, 21, 22, 24, 26.

[2] e.g. i. 36; iv. 8, 38; v. 33, &c.

[3] e.g. iv. 31, 32; vi. 11; vii. 11, 12; xiii. 34, 35. Cf. also constructions like ἐξελθόντος αὐτοῦ . . . ὑπήντησεν αὐτῷ (v. 2; cf. v. 18, 21; ix. 28; x. 17; xi. 27).

[4] e.g. i. 16; ii. 19, 20; iii. 23, 27; v. 40, 41, 42, &c.

[5] e.g. i. 41–44; iii. 9, 12, 13, 31, 32; iv. 2; v. 19, &c.

[6] e.g. ii. 18, 21; iii. 2; v. 14, 35; viii. 14, &c.

[7] e.g. ii. 6–8, 19; iv. 37; v. 13; vi. 35; ix. 37; x. 49; cf. also expressions like ἀπεστέγασαν στέγην (ii. 4); ἐξέστησαν ἐκστάσει μεγάλῃ (v. 42); ἡ ἐπιγραφὴ ἐπιγεγραμμένη (xv. 26.

For instance, 'at even when the sun did set;' 'straight-
way with haste;' 'from within, out of the heart of
men;' 'the wind ceased, and there was a great calm [1].'
It was this characteristic which gave some colour to the
theory that the Gospel was an epitome of S. Matthew
and S. Luke, a hypothesis which completely fell to the
ground when it was seen that instances of this 'duality'
occur in places where S. Mark could not possibly have
combined phrases from the other Gospels, and that it is
therefore an integral element in his style. Perhaps the
most striking as well as the commonest form which this
duality takes is the conjunction of a positive and a negative statement. Thus, 'He taught them as one having
authority and not as the scribes;' 'The sabbath was
made for man, and not man for the sabbath;' 'He cannot
stand, but hath an end;' 'But he held his peace and
answered nothing [2]:' and it would be easy to multiply
instances.

The second main characteristic of the style of S. Mark
is its peculiar vividness. The interest of the reader is
kept up by the recurrence of such phrases as 'straight-
way,' 'He began to say unto them,' and the like, which
direct the attention to a particular point of time, and so
materially assist the imagination in the realization of
the scene. But still more striking in this connexion is
the effect produced by the employment of the historic
present. Again and again in the Gospel the present
tense appears to mark the point of an incident, the centre
in which the interest of the story culminates [3]. Many
of our Lord's most striking sayings are introduced by
the words 'He saith unto them,' or a similar formula [4].
And it is noticeable how even where S. Mark appears

---

[1] i. 32; vi. 25; vii. 21; iv. 39.
[2] i. 22; ii. 27; iii. 26; xiv. 61.
[3] ii. 1-3; iii. 13-35; iv. 37, &c.
[4] ii. 8, 10, 17; iii 31; vi. 31. 50; vii. 31; viii. 12, 33, &c.

to be giving merely a condensed summary of a conver-
sation or a discourse, he presents this summary in the
form of one or two striking sentences such as would
indelibly imprint themselves on the memories of his
readers [1].

Place of
the Gospel
in the
economy
of revela-
tion.

(*d*) One word more remains to be said as to the place
which the second Gospel occupies in the 'economy of
revelation.' It contains little which is not told us elsewhere; it lacks the didactic wealth of S. Matthew, the
pathos and grace of S. Luke, the theological depth of
S. John; and yet when it is realized that it is the 'original
Gospel' *par excellence*, the earliest record of our Lord's
life of which we have any knowledge, its supreme value
becomes at once apparent. It is the foundation-stone of
the Gospel history, the necessary substructure on which
the whole fabric rests. Theology still suffers from the
effects of a former tendency to depreciate the Synoptic Gospels and especially S. Mark in comparison with
S. Paul and with S. John, a tendency which had fatal
results in many quarters, and especially in apologetics.
It seemed to many as if the figure of our Lord had become
dim and faded : they lost the power of realizing Him as
He lived and moved on the earth, and in consequence
lost also all faith in Him as a still living Being who
stands to us in the closest of all relations. The saying
of a modern writer that one of the chief problems of
education is how to present Christ to children without
'introducing Him to them in a buckram of ecclesiastical
dogma' was profoundly representative of a general feeling.
A cry arose for the historical Christ. And however irra-
tional it may have seemed to men whose faith remained
undisturbed in the midst of the prevailing distress, yet

---

[1] The use of ὅτι to introduce the 'oratio recta,' which is not a feature
peculiar to S. Mark, seems often to indicate such condensed reports ; cf.
e.g. i. 15, 37; ii. 16; iii. 22; v. 23; vi. 4, 18, 35; vii. 20; viii. 16; ix. 11,
31; x. 33; xiv. 58, 69, 71, 72.

it was on the whole a justifiable and even a noble demand. It sprang from one of the most deeply rooted aspirations of our nature, the desire to get behind traditional beliefs and systems and bring them to the test of truth itself as embodied in actual historical fact.

Unfortunately just at the time when this desire was perhaps most keenly felt, about forty years ago, the dominance of the Tübingen school of criticism prevented an appeal to the Gospel of S. Mark. It is a matter rather for regret than for surprise that when a false historical theory led critics to bring down the dates of all the Gospels well into the second century, doubts should arise about the possibility of knowing Christ as He really was. But the progress of criticism has taught us much: it has placed S. Mark in its true relation to the other Gospels, and by doing so it has presented us with a picture of our Lord, which to any unbiassed mind must bear the stamp of faithful portraiture. And the portrait which it gives is not that of a merely human Christ. For if one result has emerged more clearly than another from our increased knowledge of the origins of Christianity, it is that nothing but the most violent wrenching of the evidence can leave us with a merely human or even with an Arian Christ. Indeed in S. Mark, owing to the general absence of discourses, the miraculous element holds a larger proportionate place than it does in any of the other Gospels. And if the account which has been given of the origin of the Gospel is correct, if it represents one of the earliest cycles of apostolic preaching, then it follows that nothing can be further from the truth than to hold that our Lord appeared to His contemporaries as only a great moral teacher ; to regard the Sermon on the Mount as the sum total and essence of early Christianity and everything else, all theology properly so called, as a later accretion. To S. Mark Jesus Christ was a man ‘speaking in righteousness,’ but He was also more : He

was 'mighty   .ord of the
world and th

And so the ᴜᴜᴜᴜᴜᴜ ᴠᴀᴜᴜᴜ ᴏᴀ ᴠᴀᴜ ᴜᴜᴜᴜᴜᴜ ᴜᴜspel lies in
the fact that it forms the basis of one great branch of
the evidences for the Christian faith, the historical testimony of the Gospel records. Insistence on this point
involves no depreciation of the other three Gospels, for
each has its place, and each contributes its share to the
historical and dogmatic whole. Nor again should it lead
us to undervalue the presentation of the apostolic belief
in the Epistles, nor the validity of other branches of
evidence such as are afforded by the existence of the
Catholic Church, and by the spiritual experience of in-
dividual believers.

But to some minds at least the moral beauty of the
figure of our Lord in the Gospels will always be the
most cogent of arguments for Christianity; to many more
it will be the starting-point of their faith. From the
contemplation of Jesus as He appears in S. Mark they
will gradually advance to higher views of His person
and work : they will begin to understand the deeper
teaching of S. Paul and S. John on the mystery of the
Incarnation, until at length they come to grasp, as far
as limited humanity may, 'the measure of the stature of
the fulness of Christ.'

www.ingramcontent.com/pod-product-compliance
Lightning Source LLC
Chambersburg PA
CBHW021531270326
41930CB00008B/1195